CHRIST FOR CARNIES

CHRIST FOR CARNIES

How one family became
God's instrument of peace
in a world of lost souls

Jacquelyn Dienst

AVVENTURA PRESS

Cover and interior design by Lee Sebastiani & Lori Sebastiani, Avventura Press

Copyright © 2011 by Jacquelyn Dienst. All rights reserved.
Photos by Jacquelyn Dienst
Author photo by Mary Ann Capone

ISBN-13:
978-1-936936-01-4

Published by
Avventura Press

www.avventurapress.com

1st printing May 2011
Printed in the United States of America

Acknowledgements

First and foremost, I would like to thank my one and only Lord and Savior, Jesus Christ, and his Heavenly Father. Without them, no day, good or bad, or occasion, happy or sad, would be possible. If they did not grant me the talent to write and expose me to the right people to help nurture and develop my writing, nor direct me to the publisher who took a chance on me, this book would not exist.

Mom, Grandpa, I especially thank you for your strength, courage, and ability to overcome anything in your path. I know life was hard at many points in your life, but you truly made the best of things, even if you went without. Your gentleness, kindness, and stubbornness was a blessed mix, and I am forever grateful to have been a part of it. Mom, thank you for challenging me and encouraging me to continue to improve. Grandpa, thank you too for all that, and for trading cameras with me on that day long ago. I know you are both smiling down from Heaven as you see the joy within me to have this dream finally come true.

I want to thank my husband, John, for never letting me give up, even when times seemed impossible. You have a faith in God and a warm spirit like no other. I have never heard you say an unkind word, and you always look on the bright side. Thank you for being a source of warmth, light, and understanding. My precious children—Joseph, Rozeanna, and Hunter, my gifts from God, thank you for putting up with mommy's doing research on the computer, writing, and being crabby from pulling all-nighters. Those sessions were for you—so I could devote more time to you when you were awake. But never once did I not think of you, never once did I do something without you in mind.

I would also like to thank my family members—aunts, uncles, cousins alike, for giving me such rich material to write about over the years, and for putting up with me and my camera at every family event. I especially thank my dad, Charles R. Rivers Jr., for making my life an adventure growing up. I may not have always seen it that way at the time, but I am forever grateful for the many positives of our ever-changing lifestyle. I also thank Chrisy for being my sister as well as a good friend through thick and thin. A thank-you too, for my brothers, Jeff and Charlie, for helping to shape my character. My nieces and nephews— thank you for making me laugh and smile.

My dearest friends: Ginger, Amber, Carla, Lakendra, Stacy, Wayne, and all those I have lost touch with, thank you for making life always interesting, always helping me stand, and making every ordinary day extraordinary. Your light shines brightly in this world, and your friendship I will cherish forever.

To the Class of '87, from Deland High School in Deland, Florida, especially Bryant, Marie, Brent, Jeffery, and the many others who have stayed In contact or remembered to say hi over the years—thank you for rooting for me back then, and standing by my side now. To the new classes yet to graduate—Stand Tall, and Go Bulldogs!

My wonderful church families of the Faith Bible Church, Deltona, Florida; Sanford Christian Alliance; Sterling and Hollisterville United Methodist Churches in both Sterling and Hollisterville, PA; the incredible Pastor Pat Lee and family, and the awesome Forgiven Band–your faith, support, friendship, and guidance are true gifts, and I am proud to be a part of these congregational families.

A special thank you to Build-A-Bear, Babyland General/Cabbage Patch, WNEP, and Ryan Leckey for their kind permission and approval of pictures, copy, and video for this book. The events that took place in each establishment were vital to tell the tale, and thank you for providing those wonderful memories. Thank you to the Reo Diner and its wonderful night staff.

If I did not mention the countless people and places that stood behind me, and my wonderful readers–please know you are not forgotten in my heart. Let your light shine by performing acts of kindness every day.

Contents

Prologue 9

Growing Our Family 11

Winter Quarters 27

County Fair 45

The Mission 59

Vero Beach 73

Seminole County Fair 87

Starting Over 99

Return to the Mission 111

Georgia 125

Epilogue 133

Links 139

Prologue

At the time of our wedding on July 7th, 2007, we had it all. Nice jobs, our own apartment, an adorable daughter of our own and my older son from a former marriage. We were saving to buy our own house, and settle down somewhere between Orlando and Daytona Beach, Florida. As we said our vows in front of God and celebrated with friends and family that day, we couldn't know the crazy rollercoaster ride life had in store for us.

Not that we were strangers to adversity. John was born and raised in New Jersey, with a laundry list of crazy things in his experiences of growing up. His parents divorced when he was young, and his diligent mom worked three jobs to put herself through college and support herself and her three children. Johnny, the only boy, started his "wild child" days young, when he and his sister scaled a wooden fence at the age of two, and played hide and seek with his worried mother and the police for two hours. Since then, he had added singer in a high school band; quarterback; wrestler; roadie for Bon Jovi, and a plethora of interludes, relationships and one night stands over the years to his resumé. In short, I married the bad boy.

I too, had parents that divorced when I was young. My mother remarried when I was eight, and my stepfather adopted my brother and me. A younger brother was born when I was almost ten, a sister when I was eleven. My father made a living, it seemed, in real estate; we to move every nine to twelve months into a new home. Most of my life was spent in Florida. I was a little wild myself—my greatest escapade will only be revealed at our fiftieth high school reunion! On one adventure I skipped a day of school, hung out in a fast-food place, and ducked my mom as she went through the drive-through window. One look in the wrong direction and I'd be cooked. When my then-boyfriend and I were walking back home, we realized we wouldn't make it back in time. We gave a kindly old bus driver a sob story, and got a ride home on the bus with a little help from the rain. The loneliness I felt from moving, making friends and losing them to start all over again, making do with what I had— it all seemed to be a prelude to the strength I would need in the days to come.

How did a good girl from Florida meet and marry a wild boy from New Jersey? A mutual friend introduced us. For a time, my "bar scene" was sitting on my porch, connected to a conference line. My friend Arlene would phone people she knew and we would sit and laugh, as I drank my one glass of wine. It was fun to sit and socialize with other people, and not have the risk of being approached by a wack job or somebody drunk and confused looking for a cheap date. One particular night, Arlene brought John into the conference call. She and John had dated a few times and decided they were better off as friends. John did want a relationship, however, and said over the phone, "If I can't go out with you, then I'll just date your best friend." I laughed, and asked, "Who might that be?"

"Aren't you the one she calls sis? Then I mean you."

I laughed again. "When hell freezes over!" He calmly stated, "Look, you will not only be my girl, but I'll bet that you will be my wife."

As my grandmother said the same thing to my grandfather back in the 1930s, and they were married for almost 58 years—the devil must be pretty cold by now.

– 1 –
Growing Our Family

After a year of talking over the phone, without ever seeing each other's pictures, I arrived in New Jersey to meet him for the first time in February of 2005, and it was love at first sight. It was our faith in God that bound us, and the discovery later on that year that Rozeanna was on her way sealed the deal. No one thought he would really settle down and get married, but John, a man of his word, married me in church in early July.

John had been saved around a year earlier, when he was thirty-four, and he was looking for a change. His carefree, fly-by-night life had come to an end thanks to his cousin, who had been trying to get him to go to church for years.

John had run a gauntlet of evil ways. But deep inside he yearned to be the good man he knew he was. One day his cousin stopped by and asked him to go to church. John declined. His cousin said that he knew, one day soon, John would go—and John would call when he was ready. The next week John had a revelation, and called his cousin. He was saved that day, and set on the hardest path he had ever been on, to know the Lord.

Me? I was baptized when I was seven years old, in my native home of Springfield, Massachusetts. At the time, I heard the prayer of St. Francis, "Lord, make me an instrument of Thy peace." As I listened to the mention of a Father that would never leave me, I clung to it, and told God to please use me to do good. I wanted to please my new Father, to do something, at least in a child's mind, to win his love and affection—even though at the time I didn't understand that I already had it. When I was a late-teen, early-twenties person, however, I did stray a bit. I got together with a guy right out of high school who promised to marry me. He soon showed his true colors and beat me any chance he could get. The horrors still haunt me at the age of forty-one—but that's a different story. The miracle is that I survived, and became stronger for it.

I was twenty-one, and found myself pregnant. I packed to leave, but he caught me, beating me with a baseball bat. I lost that pregnancy as a result, and was told I would not be able to have children. So I went off the deep end. I drank myself to oblivion. It was a good six months before the Lord rattled me back to reality, by sending me a dream on New Year's Eve of walking down a path and hitting a fork in the road. One side lead to a jungle, the other, down a hill, to a green area. A group of people were there, and I went to see what they were doing. They were crying—and burying me in a glass casket. I ran up the hill, hooked a right and dove into the jungle. That woke me up, and I screamed, running out the door in pajamas and bare feet down the street to the nearest church. The message was painfully clear, and I quit drinking cold turkey. I put myself through a domestic survivor's course a few years later. When I was ready I earned an associate's degree, married for the first time in 1994, and received the greatest blessing of all when I turned 27—the birth of my first son, Joseph. Joseph, by the way, means "God Adds" and Brennan, his middle name, is Celtic, meaning, "Light from Sorrow." It would be nine years later that Rozeanna (whose name means "Love and Grace") would arrive and our journey would begin.

Our happiness in married life turned to sadness when, three days after our wedding, on July 10, 2007, a light plane carrying Nascar officials crashed into two homes in Sanford, Florida. John was witness to this. He heard the whine of the plane as it passed right over our apartment building in its descent, and then came the puff of smoke and the explosion. Dear friends of ours had lost their only daughter. Their son, Joseph's friend, was burned over ninety percent of his body. Watching the tragedy unfold on TV downstairs at my friend Amber's house, and looking out her apartment's sliding doors at the helicopters overhead was a weird experience, and a frightening one. If the plane had fallen a minute earlier, it would have wiped out the building we lived in.

The day turned worse when names of the victims were read, and a call to the pastor confirmed our fears. At that time, the little girl was unaccounted for. Since there was nothing we could do at the hospital, I had it in my head to race to the scene and hold a prayer vigil for the little girl's safe recovery. But it was not to be. It would be years before I could account for my feeling of shameful relief. Our friends' wedding gift was an offer to keep Rozeanna and

Joseph at their house while we went on our honeymoon. But we couldn't afford a honeymoon (and still haven't yet). Something we think about, every day.

Our situation spiraled downward from that point, and soon the scooter store we were running for a friend closed, booting both John and me out of a job. We were at the end of our lease and had no money to move into a new apartment, so my parents offered to let us to move back home. We did, and moved our stuff into storage, except for what we could put into the small, made-over-into-a-bedroom garage at my parents' small house. Moving back in with your parents at any age is a bit awkward; moving in when you're newly married with two year old is really strange. But we were determined to make it work, somehow. Six months, we said, at the very most, and we would be back on our feet. But we didn't know that the economy was about to sink.

I found a job the very next month with a photography company. I was thrilled. Photography is a huge part of my life—I graduated with an AS degree in both video and photography, with a touch of advertising thrown in, in 1993. I had worked over time in a variety of studios, which allowed me the luxury of taking my own pictures of my children, nieces and nephews. The photo company operated in a wholesale chain store around the state. I had to travel, but I only worked three or four days a week, at a hundred dollars a day. Johnny was still looking for another job, and Amber (my best friend in the world next to my sister and my friend Arlene) watched Rozeanna for us. Joe came to visit every other weekend, since he lived with his dad only forty five minutes from us.

But life wasn't perfect. My brothers and I have had life-long difficulty getting along, and the problems festered into adulthood. My parents were strict for good reason, with four children growing up during the drug-infested eighties. Dad was not well, and neither was Mom; she had emphysema for years, and was slowly getting worse. Not that you would know it—the strong-willed, Irish redhead was stubborn, and did what she wanted, when she wanted. As mother and daughters do, we disagreed and butted heads constantly, but I loved, and still love, my mother with all my heart. Her faith was unending. My father—we've had a hard time connecting as father in daughter over the years, but the connections we did make, and are still making, are true miracles and blessings that I am grateful for in my life.

In October of 2007 Johnny found a job with a roofing company, and both of us thought we were back on our way. We were just starting to look for another apartment by Thanksgiving, in fact, when my boss informed me that the company was shutting down for six weeks to enjoy the holidays. I was upset, but Johnny told me not to be—he was working, it was only for six weeks, I should enjoy my family, my son and our daughter. We had fun! We were part of the Deltona Days Parade, where Rozeanna, the first Toddler Miss Deltona, charmed the town. So I did enjoy that time, with the full intention of going back to work in mid January of 2008.

It was not to be.

The economy took a major nosedive in those six weeks, so much so that the company I was working for delayed opening back up with a full crew for another six weeks. I was upset to say the least. In the meantime we had to buy another car. Our little convertible finally died and was too costly to fix. John, who had never had anything financed in all his life, was suddenly trying to arrange a car payment.

We prayed to God, and seventy-two car dealers later, John found someone who took a chance on him. Our car, a 2003 Mazda Protégé, had only 30,000 miles on it. We couldn't believe our luck—and as we would find out soon enough, it was our blessing in disguise. That car would end up saving our lives.

God was a huge factor in our lives, and the only reason we were able to climb from the abyss of adversity. We had belonged to the Sanford Christian Missionary Alliance, where we were married, but the loss of four prominent members due to the airplane tragedy seemed to kill the heart of the congregation. That, combined with our moving a half hour away, found us joining Faith Bible Church, in Deltona, Florida, under the divine direction of Pastor Ron and his wonderful wife, Connie. We needed healing, and we felt alive in the church. We settled in once again to a routine, living at Mom's house and going to FBC. The Lord's part in our life was our stable anchor while everything around us was falling apart.

In January and February of 2008, I was very, very sick, as were John and Rozeanna. Double pneumonia kicked it off, followed by the flu and then bronchitis. This prevented me from going back to work, but John was making at least fifteen dollars an hour and we were starting to save money again, even with the car payment. At the end of February I was still sick, and frustrated with not knowing what in the world was going on. My mom gave me the first clue when she said,

"It must be your time of the month—you're awfully crabby."

I shook my head no, and she remarked that I must be getting ready to have it. This left me wondering, because

Mother Nature visited me like clockwork. I went to the calendar in my room and flipped back one page, then another, and gasped. Either I was going through an early change of life, or I was pregnant. How could that be? When Rozeanna was born, the doctors told me that only one of my Fallopian tubes working. It would be a million to one shot to have another child.

A quick visit to the store and the bathroom confirmed my suspicion. How could it be? My eyes lifted upward. John and I had talked about having another child, but only when we were back on our feet. I sat on the bed, listening to my parents and my visiting grandmother talking. I suddenly felt like a teenager who just discovered she was pregnant. There were enough problems with so many people in the house—what right did I have to bring in one more? It was up to God for sure this time. John was thrilled when I told him, though he was a little nervous. I told him that I was happy, and mostly, I was. Apprehensive though, about telling my folks...which didn't go too well. I was called irresponsible—which, I guess in one way, was deserved. But in the end, Boo (the baby's nickname because he sort of snuck up on us) was already on the way. What could be done? Abortion was out of the question. To me, it is murder in the first degree, and wasn't going to happen. Somehow, we would survive, and John and I looked to the Lord to guide us. We weren't too worried, as long as John kept working, and I would work as long as I could.

All that changed two weeks later, when John came home early. I was concerned that he was sick. He wasn't sick, but he did go and lie down. I immediately made him a cup of coffee, and became really worried when he didn't want any. John and coffee went together like a hand and glove. If they needed people for experimental caffeinated IV's, John would be their guinea pig.

"I was laid off," he said simply, staring at the ceiling. "A lot of us were."

A lot was an understatement. There was a total of four thousand workers in three counties now out of work.

That was the start of a trend for everyone in the construction industry. Between companies' cutting corners on labor costs and the economy, the only work a skilled man could get was doing repairs for the half-baked job that the first crew did. I always thought this would cost the company more money in the long run than doing it right the first time, but I was no corporate exec, and no big shot was going to listen to a worker bee's wife. So we were stuck with the six weeks of work, then six weeks of lay off, then work again routine for the entire year.

The Lord, as always, worked in mysterious ways. I worked every other weekend until my fifth month of pregnancy, when I was placed on bed rest. How one can do bed rest when a very active two year old is with you is anyone's guess. Roze and I watched a lot of TV and videos that year. I knew Sesame Street all over again. Yet, somehow, the Lord always came through, either with a heartfelt donation from a friend, or someone's suddenly paying back a debt on the day our car payment was due, small miracles we constantly prayed for. My parents were also big supporters, helping us here and there with insurance, car payment and storage unit. If not for their emotional and financial support, we probably would not have survived the winter to come.

The bigger I got during the pregnancy (which was hard, thanks to gestational diabetes and other complications) the harder John looked for work. God always provided, from contracts to mowing grass, to fixing soffits on an old lady's home. We grew closer, praying together as a family, and reading the Bible till we fell asleep at night.

October was a month of excitement, when we thought we were on the way up once more. My due date was coming fast, it was October the tenth, and John had been working steady since the end of August. We thought the worst was over, but looking back, I know it was just the calm before the storm.

Hunter Wolfe, ("To Actively Seek," "A Great Spirit") named for a long ago ancestor, came into the world early in the morning weighing an astonishing eleven pounds, a whole twenty-one days before he was due. For those of you who've been counting, Boo's actual due date was Halloween.

When a child comes into the world by a planned C-section, he is usually in the neonatal unit a bit longer than most other newborns. But this was not the case for Hunter. John had given up his spot in the unit, letting Amber, one of Hunter's godmothers in instead. John finally got to hold his son the next morning, but only for a few moments. His only son—the one who was to carry on the family name, and the first boy born in forty years on his side of the family. The nurse was called when we noticed the baby wasn't breathing very well and had a bluish tinge around his mouth. It was an hour later that the pediatrician came in and told us Hunter was not well. He had a heart murmur, and his lungs were not clearing as they should. His breathing was poor. John got to see his son through the glass when I went in to feed him. So many leads were stuck on Hunter to monitor every function, and all I could do was push milk through a tube, and touch his little hand. However excruciating it was for me not to hold Hunter, it was doubly so for John, watching worriedly through the glass. We both silently wondered if our blonde-haired, blue-eyed angel would become exactly that.

A call to Pastor Ron was in order, to tell him that the baby the congregation had come to love before he ever arrived might be going "home" sooner than anyone ever planned. It was on Sunday afternoon that I was surprised with a visit from the Pastor and his wife. We were told the entire congregation had activated the prayer chain, and had been praying for Hunter since the phone call was made. They had also held a special prayer for him during service, and we continued to pray in that hospital room. The decision to move Hunter to a children's hospital down the road was to be made in the morning.

I sat in the waiting room with a double pump under a blanket, until they told me I could "board" with the hospital in a private room. People brought me food from church, and my friend kept Rozeanna with her. John was killing himself, working, then staying the night, sleeping in a chair beside me, reading the Bible and praying until we fell asleep holding hands. Then I would have to wake and use the breast pump to feed Hunter again.

John was gone when I awoke. He saw past my façade, knew my pain, and watched from a corner as I cried after touching and singing to our little man, who was now under yellow lights to cure the jaundice that ran rampant through his body, on top of all else.

Monday morning brought great anxiety when nine o'clock came. We made phone calls from my room every half hour, only to grow frustrated with the fact that the pediatrician hadn't yet arrived. Time ticked on endlessly, and the phone rang off the hook with worried relatives and friends wanting updates. Hunter looked no better when I went to visit him, but the little guy did respond and calm when my voice was heard.

Finally, around 3 p.m., my sister called for the umpteenth time to ask what the heck was going on. I was about to reply that there was no change, when my door opened. The words stuck in my throat as my sister repeatedly called my name and asked what was wrong.

"Are you Hunter's mother?" asked the man who had entered my room.

I could only nod, hearing my sister in my other ear, getting more frantic.

"I am the hospital chaplain," the man said, coming farther into the room. He wore no smile.

"Please....come with me."

And just like that, he walked out the door.

"Ah....The hospital chaplain walked into my room," I said. "I have to go."

"WHAT??" My sister cried. "Don't they do that when things are going bad?"

"I...don't know. I have to go." I dropped the phone and ran, as fast as my sewn-together body would allow me.

The chaplain was down the hall already, at the door. My room was the first on the left, just past the nurses' desk, next to the doors. Beyond the doors was the nursery. I could see, just inside the window, a huge machine set up near my son, and two doctors and a nurse running frantically around the room. It was enough to make me sink against the wall.

"Oh...GOD...." I thought. "They're giving him last rites." My steps were slow and heavy as I walked toward the doors that the chaplain held open. I had visions of John running off the roof in grief after I made the phone call...if I could make it at all. Stepping through the doors, I took a deep breath and closed my eyes a moment.

"Thank you Heavenly Father, for the time we had with Hunter," I whispered. "At least, John got to hold his son, and look upon his face for a few precious moments. Thank you Lord, for that."

Then, I opened my eyes to look at my son, who was barely making any movement. The doctors and nurses were still hurrying around, and I saw the pediatrician heading my way.

"God, give me strength, please." I whispered. And got ready for the news.

But it was not the news I was expecting.

"Mrs. Dienst," the pediatrician said, coming around the corner. "I want to tell you..."

"That my son won't live," I finished quietly.

Silence.

"No...that I have never seen such a miraculous recovery as I have just seen in the last twenty-four hours," the woman said. "The doctors are confirming. But everything is good. The onset of pneumonia is gone, the breathing rate is good, and his lungs are clear. The heart murmur is even fading, and the jaundice is clearing up," she replied.

My eyes flew open, and traveled to the chaplain.

"I wanted you to see for yourself," he said, smiling. "Your son is a miracle. Shall we pray? I wanted to pray in sight of your son."

Tears of joy, tears of happiness, flowed, and all I could do was nod my head. The lump in my throat was too great. Just then, as if in confirmation, Hunter let out a wail that got all the other babies crying with him in chorus.

It was the sweetest sound I ever heard.

Within twenty-four hours, my friend picked up Hunter and me, and for the first time, I carried him into my parent's home, where the four of us were reunited. Joseph came soon after to visit, happy as a king that he had now a sister and a brother.

Once again, our happiness did not last. On November fifth, his birthday, John came home from work, straight to a phone call that the company had folded, and his job was again defunct. He didn't even have a chance to take off his coat. This was not the way to spend your thirty-ninth birthday at all. The little celebration of lasagna and birthday cake instantly became next day's leftovers, as our appetites were again ruined. The job hunt was on once more, just a few weeks before Christmas.

Christmas was going to be a small affair, but we didn't care much. Rozeanna was small and Joseph was old enough to understand we didn't have much money. Besides, he had gifts coming from both sets of grandparents, aunts, uncles and his father. We did receive a blessing, however, when a kind stranger called the church, and the dear pastor gave him our name on Christmas Eve. The stranger met us at the local chain store to go Christmas shopping for our kids. He felt moved to bless someone, and Rozeanna and Joe ended up with more than they thought they would.

At the church, Hunter was a bit of a celebrity. The people who had prayed in earnest for the little guy couldn't wait for us to walk through the door on Sunday. Hunter had become a community baby, it seemed, going first from my arms to Ms. Connie, then to each deaconess, and to every other lady in the place. All of the children there were just as loved, and parents lost their kids to a sea of hugs and kisses from the moment they walked in, not seeing them until fellowship after service.

We were honored when the Christmas pageant rolled around. Everyone was involved in some way. Rozeanna was on stage with the young children her age, holding little baby dolls and singing "Happy Birthday, Dear Jesus." John sang in the chorus, Joseph videotaped the entire event, and I took the photographs. Our proudest moment came when Hunter, then only two-and-a half months old, played the role of Baby Jesus in the live Nativity, "The Open Door."

I cried with joy when the chorus broke into "Silent Night," and the children playing Joseph, Mary and Baby Jesus marched up the aisle to take their places on stage. It reminded me of the days when, as a child at Christmas parties at my grandparents, my oldest cousin would read the story of Bethlehem while the parents cleaned up and packed the cars. Then, in our coats, led by Grandpa in a candlelight procession, we would surround a handmade, handed-down, Nativity scene from old Ireland on the snow covered lawn, singing "Silent Night" while Grandpa laid baby Jesus into the manger. The black canvas night dotted with diamond stars held witness as it had been so long ago. A neighborhood gang destroyed that lovely heirloom one Christmas morning, and the tradition ended until Grandpa could find another Nativity where the Baby was removable. It never happened...but standing there, watching my son be placed in the life-sized manger as the chorus sang, I felt pride and joy along with that touch of Heaven, and knew that Grandpa, who died in 1999, was watching.

It was a wonderful party that night, full of good times, family and friends, one that would stay in my memory for all eternity. If I had known at that time it would be the last for many years, maybe I would have been a little more grateful for that family togetherness.

John tried to find another job without success. My parents, despite their love, were getting a bit antsy at times. It was understandable; there were already too many people in their small house, and now, one more had arrived. John had brought up something that he had mentioned from time to time, about how he traveled with the carnival for a few years, and how there were families that traveled. The one thing that he wanted was to keep us all together. It was something I did not want, with my history of moving around. I wanted that little white house with a picket fence, growing roots, grandkids-going-to-the same-school-you-did type of life. I had had it briefly with Joseph's father, but it doesn't last when neither person is really ready. Now, at age thirty-nine, with three kids and a new partner for life, I wanted things to change.

But, as I was about to find out, what we have planned is not always God's plan, and sometimes, what we want is not what God wants for us. Even though we may not understand at the time, or even understand at all until we meet our Maker, we should thank God for His wisdom in knowing what is best for us better than we do. Sometimes, it is because we have to walk through the fire to be brought to a higher level of maturity; sometimes, it's because we need to simply understand people. Most of the time, it is because we need to be humbled, and be grateful for what we have, and to understand that from the time we are born, we have all we need for this world. In our case, it would become a mixture of all the above.

On December 31, 2008, John pulled me outside to my parents' screen porch to talk and sip the one glass of wine I allowed each of us to celebrate.

"I got a job the other day," he began, taking my hand and kissing it. "I hope you are proud of me."

"Of course I am," I told him. "Why wouldn't I be?"

John smiled, but glanced downward, in the way he does when he's about to say something that I won't like.

"What is it?" I asked anxiously.

"The job I got....It's with a traveling carnival," he admitted.

I sat back, slightly stunned. "What?" I finally asked. "How can..?"

"You won't be going with me," John said. I want you to stay here with your mom. Find a job, have your friends and family help you. Be safe."

I couldn't speak for a few moments. Hunter was only two months old. Rozeanna was a daddy's girl. And—we had not been married for even a year and a half.

"How long?" I whispered.

John looked away, then up at the moon.

"Almost a year," he murmured. "Thanksgiving."

"I have to do what I can for my family," he said after several moments of silence.

I only nodded. His mind was made up—and I managed a weak smile.

"OK. I was a single mom for five years after the divorce. Who is to say I can't do it again?" I asked him.

"But you're not single," John protested, kissing my hand. "I love you. You are my wife. We will be together again, I promise."

I nodded, and smiled, but my moist eyes betrayed all my emotion.

"When do you leave?" I asked.

"Two weeks. Can you drop me off?" he asked. "You need to keep the car."

"Sure," I nodded, glancing up at the moon.

My tiny world had begun to fall apart, and my parents were less than thrilled with the idea. It was, in their mind, abandonment. Who could blame them? They were doing as parents do—protecting their daughter, their grandchildren. It was no secret to anyone that I was completely unhappy and a bit dispirited at this point.

"You will not be alone," the Pastor promised, when we told him that Sunday. "John, you will have a phone, right?"

John shook his head. "Soon as I can get one."

"Well, from what I understand you will be in Florida until the end of April. We will make sure you have one by then."

John nodded, grateful that the Church, such a part of our lives already, was going to be involved.

We just didn't know how much.

What does this have to do with Christ for Carnies? Everything. For it is said, to truly understand another, you must first walk in his shoes. To know John and me is to know why Christ for Carnies was born in the first place; to know how the tiny mission seeds we planted on January 15, 2009, would bring God and his Word to a world that few know exists, souls lost in a place that could rival a third-world country, right in America's backyard. My family became God's instrument of peace in the middle of what's been nicknamed "The Devil's Playground." We held fast to our faith and our love for each other despite temptation, despite the danger, despite the world, who wanted us to give up. Through everything, Christ is indeed for carnies. Christ is for us all.

Christ for Carnies

Pastor Ron and some members of the FBC Youth Group passing out blankets

– 2 –
WINTER QUARTERS

January 15, 2009. The day dawned clear, with azure in the sky and a bright yellow sun. It was reasonably warm with a light breeze blowing. Winter is the most-looked-forward-to time of year in Florida. (It really seems to have two seasons—summer, and not-so-summer.) A cold snap works its way in sometimes, sending the shorts-and-tee-shirt Floridians running for our jackets and sweaters; the snowbirds, those from up North to escape the snow, just giggle. Today was not one of those days, since the mild temperature made outdoor activities a pleasant experience. For most people, anyhow.

I had to help my husband pack up his belongings—not much—in the one bedroom the four of us shared. John spent most of the afternoon holding Hunter and sitting with Roze, watching her favorite video for the millionth time. At noon, John said goodbye to my parents, who mumbled their farewells, and we packed Roze and Hunter into the car, backed out of the drive, and were on our way.

Orlando was about a forty-five minute drive, the carnival, fifteen minutes past that. We arrived at the carnival office just about one o'clock, and I waited for John to go into the office and fill out his paperwork as the kids slept in the backseat. To pass the time, I looked at the boneyard of carnival rides scraping various heights in the sky, and the myriad trailers and buildings beyond. There was a train, I'd been told, one of two left in the United States that still carried a carnival, but I couldn't see it. The carnival life, romanticized in times past, was a far cry from romantic in reality. John came out, a smile on his face, and I tried to smile back.

"OK, I need to get to work now," he said excitedly, leaning over to kiss me. "We are going to be here for the next month. So I can come home on the weekends, for now."

I nodded.

"Hey...." he said, tipping up my chin so I could meet his deep, deep blue eyes and that charming smile that won my heart. "It's going to be OK. We are going to be OK. I swear to you, and I swear to God. I love you."

"I know," I said, trying to keep the tremor out of my voice. "I....Wake the kids and say goodbye, OK? You need to go."

John leaned over and gave me a long, deep kiss. "I want to keep that with me all week."

"Me too, " I whispered.

The kids were awakened, and Rozeanna stared in wide-eyed wonder at the different rides within her view, while Hunter just stared with the same blue eyes as his father's.

John gave them both a kiss, explaining that he had to go to work, and would see them again soon. Then, with a last smile, he walked backwards to the gate, which opened on the dirt road that started this new path of life for us.

I backed out, calmly brought the kids home, gave them a bath, read to them, and rocked both to sleep. My mom watched with concerned eyes, but said nothing for a while. It wasn't until after everyone in the house was sound asleep, and the lights were out, that I went outside into my car. I was struck silly how cold it had turned, the temperature going down all through the day, just like my spirits. A cold snapped had come, breaking forty-year-old records in some places. I shivered as I climbed into the cold car, bowed my head to say silent prayers—and burst into heart wrenching tears instead, with no one but God and the stars to listen.

God heard my pain.

Mom found me in the car early that morning, asleep over the steering wheel. She told me quietly that the baby had woken her, and I had to marvel at this woman before me. She had been sick for years with emphysema, twenty-one years to be exact, with an oxygen tank trailing her for almost ten. I remember the day she was diagnosed, and how little time the doctors given her. But Mom, a tall, good-looking Irish red head with fiery green eyes and spirit to match, told the doctors that she and God had a pact, and as long as she kept her faith, He would let her see her grandchildren be born. It would be almost seven years after that statement that Joseph, the eldest, was born, and another twelve when Hunter was born. She had told me on seeing him, that this was it—her last grandchild. I asked her how she knew? She had three other children younger than I was. They could have plenty more.

She told me that if there was another child, it would be a girl, and be born after she had died. But, Mom being Mom, she warned me not to name the baby after her. That remarkable woman with steadfast faith had been concerned for her children. I shouldn't be surprised—I would go to the ends of the earth for my kids, and I was one of hers.

As a single mom, a daily routine with one child is tough enough, but manageable. Routine, with a newly-turned three-year-old and a three month old, is impossible. But somehow I was ready to take that challenge, to prove to the world I would not fail, that God was beside me, and that my husband was doing everything he could for his family. My hands were free thanks to the sling and front pack I carried Hunter in, and Roze was at least old enough to follow directions in reasonable order.

A phone call came, and changed our whole world.

"Hi, hon," It was John. I was happy just hearing his voice. "I need you to do me a favor. Please get some blankets for me out here. Sheets for the beds, and some sweaters."

I raised a brow. "They don't have any?" I asked him.

"No, we have to supply our own," he replied.

"Well, what about heat? Don't they have any on that train?"

His next words nearly killed me.

"No," he replied. "I shorted out the electric grill, in fact—my roommate and I turned it on and opened it up for heat. We're some of the lucky ones, though. Some of these guys don't even have sheets on the beds."

I couldn't speak, I couldn't cry, I couldn't scream. I could only think, "Thanks be to God, John didn't freeze to death."

"OK....I will. I'll be there tonight." A moment's pause.

"How many people are out there, John?"

"Around three hundred and fifty," John replied. "I have to go, hon, back to work. I borrowed someone's cell, and walked to the bathroom. I can't be gone very long. I love you," he said, and hung up.

"I love you too," I said, but to the dial tone.

Mom was at her computer, her favorite pas time, selling books on E-Bay.

"Mom," I said softly, sinking on the couch. "It's so cold out...John shorted out the small grill he has, using it for heat."

The click-clack of keys stopped, and she turned in her seat to face me.

"Really?" she asked.

"Yeah. I need to take him some blankets, some sheets. Something." I said.

Mom nodded, and looked around. Dad was in the bedroom, resting from a headache. She tilted her head towards me, motioning me to come closer.

"Let me get into my bedroom," she whispered, "I will give you some money. Get him a heater, and a sleeping bag, or something," she whispered. Aloud, she said, " Go into the spare bedroom, and looked in the closet. There are a few blankets and sheets you can bring him.

I nodded my head, gave her a hug, and went in there, to find what she was talking about. Dad came in to make sure I got the right stuff.

The whole thing bothered me. I went out into my room, where Hunter was taking a nap, and Rozeanna was watching a movie. I had the phone still in my hand. John would be taken care of, but what about the rest? I couldn't fathom it. Before I knew it, I called the Pastor, and heard his comforting voice on the line. I told him about what happened, and his voice filled with immediate concern.

"I can't stand the thought," I told him. "All those people, so cold out there. I know how cold it was. Is there something we can do?"

Of course, his first answer was to pray for guidance, which we did then and there. After that, the Pastor and I started talking about possibilities. Calling everyone in the congregation might produce a good amount of warm bedding, but not enough for all. What would we do when we ran out? The air was still cold, and it was going to get severely cold for the next few nights.

"Maybe we can make some phone calls to some organizations," I suggested as God popped the idea into my head. The Pastor promised me the church would be behind whatever I wanted to do. I thanked him and hung up the phone, getting to work. There was only a small window of time—videos only last so long before a child gets restless, and Hunter would only nap for a little while. The Internet and I soon got to work. The worst thing people could say was no, and just like it was when we were buying the Mazda, I did not take no for an answer.

God pulled the impossible out of thin air.

Within two hours I found a kind spirit in the community relations coordinator for an organization called Harvest Time in Sanford. They did much for the community, from offering low-priced groceries and other items to those in need, to providing bedding and toiletry items for organizations. I told him the situation, and couldn't believe my ears at the response when I asked if he could spare some of those items.

"How big a truck do you want me to fill?" the man on

the other end of the line said.

"Really?" I asked, simply amazed.

"Tell you what. I will fill as many cars as you can get here by five today, or I will fill a twenty-four foot truck. Will that suffice?"

A definite yes, with a few details followed, and then I was back on the line with the Pastor.

"Praise God," said the Pastor. "You have my van, and we have your car. I'll make a few phone calls to the church deacons, and you make a few too, OK?"

"You got it," and the phone calls began.

The time was then around noon. At four o'clock, my car, the Pastor's minivan, and three more vehicles—a truck, an SUV, and another car—pulled up to the back lot. The Pastor took care of the paperwork details, while the rest of us began pulling sheets, blankets, comforters, pillows, pillow cases, towels and facecloths out of huge boxes. Rozeanna giggled as I all but buried her brother and hers, from the floorboards up, between two of them. Trunk and passenger seat were also filled. We packed the other vehicles in a similar fashion.

The Pastor had me call John when five o'clock rolled around.

"Tell everyone not to go anywhere, John, and wait for us to come in," I said. When he asked what was going on, I just grinned with happiness. "Oh, just wait and see."

Amazingly, it took us only an hour to pack our little convoy, and we were on our way, the little green Mazda Protégé in the lead, weaving through rush hour traffic, blasting Christian music, me singing at the top of my lungs.

Halfway there, I had to laugh, then scold, my three year old, as she flung out facecloths, saying, "One for me, and one for the birds. Fly, fly, fly!" and letting the wind snatch them from the car window. Although I was glad she was learning the concept of giving, we couldn't afford to lose what we had packed. Happily she got the message when I told her that all this was for daddy—and she hugged the nearest pile.

At the train, a line of curious people stood waiting for this mysterious gift, shivering in the cold and suspicious of our intent. They craned their necks as a line of cars hit the dirt road. I jumped out and hugged John, who was amazed and delighted at the same time. He then shook the Pastor's hand and hugged him, as well as those who came along to help.

"Jackie, this is Scott, the coordinator for my boxcar," John said, introducing me. I grinned at the number of the boxcar—the date we were married, in fact. Shaking Scott's hand, I told him what we had done.

"Spread the word," the Pastor said. "We have enough for everyone."

Along with the drivers had come some of the church youth group to help, and their eyes were opened to a world they had never seen before. People, some still covered in grease since they had not yet seen a shower, popped their heads out from the train and from their bunk house doors. Soon, the small line in the cold grew, and everyone waited patiently for their turns.

"Thank you," was chorused over and over again. "I'm not going to freeze tonight!" others exclaimed. Still others said they were grateful that God had not forgotten them. The Pastor prayed for everyone, took some pictures, and then he and the others left. I stayed behind. John was busy walking with Rozeanna for a bit and holding Hunter, while

I continued coordinating the provisions. Extras were stored in compartments on the train.

As in the story of fish and loaves, everyone who would come aboard for the next three months was sent to Scott for a care packet, and anyone who left passed on his gift to someone who could use it after it was laundered.

One of the carnies, a shy, older man who humbly took his blankets and other items, touched my heart so that I started to weep.

"I thought I was going to freeze to death," he said quietly. "I had every set of clothing I owned on, and was still cold. I had forgotten the warmth of a blanket. Thank you."

I could only gave him a hug.

John and his roommate received a special blessing—a heater for their room, and for John, a green arctic sleeping bag, which he still owns and uses today.

That simple act of kindness earned me, the kids and all who came respect out there on the carnies' home ground, and men who had forgotten that decent people exist were suddenly smiling and tipped their baseball caps at me. I smiled happily, praising God all the way home, and dropping wearily into bed.

The next few days were spent caring for the kids, doing chores, and finding other organizations to donate items. Canned food was a priority, as was a simple tool we all take for granted— the can opener. Portable stoves were needed, along with toiletry items such as toilet paper, shampoo, soap and deodorant. Prayers had begun every night, with me turning from my own needs to the needs of the men and women who brought joy to so many others at county, city, and state fairs.

During next two weeks I made trips almost daily, always

with the car packed, bearing gifts from Freecycle items to donations of food and cases of water, and even a hundred and twenty pairs of good jeans. The outpouring of generosity was fantastic.

The beginning of February brought another blessing, as the workers began setting up for the first of six Florida festivals in Osceola County. Our tax refunds had come in, and thanks to the addition of Hunter, brought in a few thousand dollars. I was in my glory—I had an unlimited supply of gas for the trips, which were an hour each way. I also had something more important. Telling Scott that there were a few more donations than there actually were, John and I unanimously decided to tithe our percentage by helping out in every way that we could. The ministry we had created still didn't have a name, but we weren't too worried. One would come, in time.

In the meantime, my weekends were filled. Either John visited our house, or we stayed with John, though not in a way that anyone really wanted to. We slept in the car, the kids and I. John slept in the passenger seat. One night, when he was not feeling well and needed to stretch out his back, I sent him to his "room" on the train. In his place, to make sure no one bothered us, was Scott, who had become fast friends with the kids and me. Now, I wasn't a stupid mom—I never let my kids out of my sight. I didn't know anyone in the carnival very well, and I wouldn't risk anything happening to my children. Scott and I spent the night fogging up the windows with laughter, as we talked and told each other jokes most of the night. In many ways it was like a campout with a friend, an experience I so enjoyed as a kid.

Close to the opening day of the first fair, a donation

came in from an anonymous person. It was a great feeling; our little ministry without a name was running strong. The Pastor and Ms. Connie gave great direction, and the local grocery stores, department stores, and individuals donated gift cards for food, toiletry items, and more. This cash donation was something different.

I was very disturbed to find that now that the carnies were working, they were responsible for their own food. (Meals were provided by some very sour looking women with attitudes to match when the carnies worked on the rides between seasons in their "Winter Quarters.") The nearest grocery store was five miles down the road. Very few of the carnies owned cars, and those that did charged the others at least ten dollars a trip there and back. This was just ludicrous to me. Many of these men had children and were paying child support and other expenses. Some had children in the care of a relative, as in the case of a couple that we grew to know. In the end, our little green Mazda became a charity-run taxi.

This gift was a blessing, and I took each boxcar and bunkhouse coordinator to the dollar store. There they bought soap, shampoo, toilet paper and other items that their car would need. There was enough left over to bring in a surprise for the workers when they came in from setting up the rides: thirty pizzas, all delivered, and soda enough for all.

The workers were totally surprised, but a few approached as the pizza man came in. Many asked, "How much?" and were shocked at the answer.

"Join me in prayer," I said quietly, and reached out my hands. Not one person turned away, though some had said they hadn't prayed in a long time.

"God loves you, enough that he gave his only Son, to save you, to save those who believe. If you believe in your heart, then it will be easy," I told them.

"I have never seen anything like this," one ride operator (called a ride jock) said. "Why did you do this?"

"Well, I didn't do this," I told them. "God provided a way, and gave me the idea. He used me to get his message across—that he loves all of you, and so do I, as a sister in Christ."

"Of all the days in my life, this one day I will never forget," said the ride jock.

The Pastor also visited often, giving John, who was quietly battling depression from being away from his family, a boost to his spirit. The list of people that would seek out John and me to pray with or for them, or ask the Pastor something, or, better yet, ask to be brought to church for the first time, grew in leaps and bounds.

The Pastor came out early that Sunday morning, and stood talking with John, Scott and me for a good twenty minutes before we drove off, happily, with a group of people. I could take one more passenger—John squeezed in between our kids in the back, and a polite, nice, young fellow named Chad got in. It was a special day for us; we were becoming official members of the church at long last, and we had several people to help celebrate it with us. We were not the only ones to join, which made it all the sweeter.

For Scott, it was his second trip to the Faith Bible Church, and he looked forward to every Sunday. He and John would meet after work outside, since the weather was warming up to a tolerable level. There they would read and talk about the Bible, a sort of informal Bible study. They vowed to maintain it throughout the season, and opened the discussion to all who wished to join.

Scott gave his testimony to how he came to God, as did a few others that were there.

"I was in jail for drugs," he had said, "And knew I was going to be in jail for a long time. I had screwed up. One of the books I was able to get hold of was the Bible, and I read the book of Job. I identified with him." Michael paused, as many watched, mesmerized. "For the first time in four years, I got down on my knees, and asked God to help me. If He could help me get out of this mess, I would never touch another drug, and try to help others get off of this stuff." Scott paused again, glancing upward, as if asking for strength for the next sentence.

"It was a day later that my attorney pulled me in for a conference. She told me about a program that would put me on probation and community service. I cried, right there in front of her, and said, 'Thank you Jesus. I will follow you.' I wondered for what purpose I was spared a twenty-plus year jail sentence." He smiled then, and glanced at John, who gave him thumbs up.

"I think I got that answer last month, when I met John. His first assignment was to make up his bunk, and put his things away. I introduced myself as the coordinator, and told him point blank that I run a tight ship, and if did drugs, he could march right back out the door. John shook my hand and told me, 'No problem, man. I don't do drugs anymore. Not since my twenties, in fact. Besides, I'm a Christian, and I'm only here to support my wife and kids, because roofing is bust.' That is when I knew I had misjudged John because of his tattoos and all. I knew I had found a brother."

His words earned thunderous applause.

The Pastor got up then, and thanked Scott for giving

his testimony. He then announced that the mission we had started was growing, and welcomed again those who had come to visit from the carnie world.

Bible study and visits would continue for at least a week more, until the first carnival was to open. In the meantime, other duties were performed, including the impromptu taxi service I had going with the Mazda. Rides to the bus stop, grocery store, department stores, laundromat, and even a car dealer were given. Everyone who rode, happily gave a "tip" for the ride, which paid for the gas, paid for lunch, paid to keep the car running in tip-top shape.

My trips didn't stop, as I continued, with the help of the Church, to advocate for these men and women, asking individual stores for gift certificates to buy food. John was taken care of, because I'd make sure he'd eat and had supplies for the days I would not be around. The Salvation Army store a few miles down the road proved to be a real gem. There are two sections in this particular store, one for the normal way the organization operates—placing out goods at decent prices—and a smaller section, where items that had been on the shelves for a certain time would be dumped in a bin and sold at the amazing price of a dollar a bagful.

When carnies are in Winter Quarters, they are fed three meals a day, but they must be eaten at certain times by everyone on the ground. If you missed the times, if you disobeyed the rules, or ticked off the women who served you— you were on your own. The women's disapproving looks as I smiled and nodded at them made me kind of sad inside as I brought boxes of food and cases of water to hand out to those who needed some. The other thing about Winter Quarters was the sad, sad pay. While working a full, forty-hour shift, and sometimes on the weekend, the men and women make only around five dollars a day. Yes, that's not an hour, that is a DAY. With taxes taken out of that, to boot. The final pay for a week? A whole $25 dollars. I asked how they could possibly get away with this, and the answer was, "Well, their room and board costs so much. We could take it all and pay them nothing, but we are being generous."

On the road, they are paid a salary of $250 to $300 a week before taxes and provided lodging, but are responsible for their own food and their own laundry. A perfect racket, since the majority of the carnies did not have vehicles. Often on the road there was no public transportation, and many would have to rely on a taxi, or pay someone an exorbitant amount to be carpooled. Or, they'd spend it right back into the carnival. Many more still had child support taken right out of their pay, and were left with anywhere from $25 to $80 for the week.

All of this, of course, was upsetting to my family and friends, who questioned John's wisdom. Things like, "He just doesn't want to be here, he can't deal with the kids," and "He just doesn't want to get a real job,' were said. A few folks even tried to encourage me to claim abandonment, to increase my assistance level. I flatly refused, saying that, somehow, Jesus would provide, and I would not break the law and commit fraud in the system. John hadn't abandoned me, I said staunchly.

Though, in my heart, I felt alone, and grew lonelier each day.

Finally, the opening day of the first of six Florida fairs had arrived, and the entire world was about to take a wild and wacky turn on the rollercoaster of life.

I loaded this double stroller with water for the carnies

- 3 -
County Fair

The Osceola County Fair is pretty large by most standards, and it was in full swing when I pulled in to park and walked through the gate. I was allowed in for free, taking my sister and my friend in with all of our children. There was a promise of John's spending time with us later that evening—he was still at WQ, as it was now called, fixing up a carnival favorite called the Zipper. I was to go back around seven to pick him up. I had Joseph with me this Friday night, too. Everyone knew who I was, and they were grateful. I kept reminding them that it was not me, exactly, but it was God who provided, and the church was involved. In no way was I going to take all the credit for what was truly a team effort.

I had heard about another church that had been at the fair for the past few years, giving out soup, sandwiches, coffee and tea to the workers out of love. They also had a tent with a booth that offered contributions of shoes, clothes, blankets and other items. It sat behind the Big Wheel and the Himalaya rides. A smiling lady in her mid-forties led the group, and welcomed the help. We sat down and talked awhile, as the kids played in the tent. I was glad for my kids to have some exercise; their days had been filled with riding in their car seats, sleeping in them, and being dragged from this appointment to that store for the last month. Life did not stop for me, since Rozeanna had been diagnosed with a speech issue that needed to be resolved with therapy twice a week. Hunter, only five months old, still had doctors' appointments every month, and chores were a never ending thing. Tensions were beginning to ride high with my friends and family, who continued to try to convince me to claim abandonment, even temporary, to get more help. Also, there were a few times I broke a play date, or other activity, to tend to the needs of others. No good deed goes unpunished, and in many eyes the gavel of judgment was already struck down.

I thought that maybe this day would help me make some kind of amends. Free entry and free rides was a good peace offering; at least, that's what I thought. I never stopped loving my friends and family, and respected their thoughts and opinions. However, I was not going to divorce or claim abandonment from a man who was killing himself to make the worst pay in history in a depressed economy to support us. What kind of wife would I be, and what kind of hypocrite before God would I be, who I took my vows for richer, for poorer, for better and worse? Besides, Rozeanna was happy; she got to see her father, and Hunter was making a few connections with his father, so important in a baby's life.

The decision was made that the lady and I would join forces as often as we could throughout Florida to provide for the workers, maybe for their whole seasonal run.

"I would like to do something for teardown," the kind lady stated, whom I shall call Wendy.

"What is teardown?" I asked.

"Well, when the last day of the fair arrives, these people work it all day long, just like every day of the fair. Only, when the lights go out and the time comes to an end, they begin tearing down the rides, and don't stop until they are done." Wendy's brown eyes met my own, and were troubled. "Sometimes, it is not until four or five in the afternoon on Monday, or later, when they are finished."

I was taken aback by this information. "I had no idea," I managed to say.

"No one really does," Wendy replied. "How would we? Think about it. If you visited the fair before, and I am sure you have, did you notice how tired and drawn these people are? Or the sadness in their eyes? The look of the lost soul? Or did you just ride the ride, and go on your merry way?"

I couldn't say anything, just nodded.

"Some people actually say, "What's the deal with this job? Any idiot can push a button to operate a ride." Wendy stated."But if they only knew. If they really knew, and remembered that they are people too. Yeah, a lot of them have a bad rap in their past. You can't trust all of them, just like you can't trust everyone in the world. But God loves them, and is here for them too. Many just seem to forget that, in the midst of having fun."

I nodded again, nearly moved to tears of shame.

Wendy changed the subject, sensing my onset of tears. "Have you thought of a name yet for the mission?"

I looked at her and replied, :I think you just gave me the answer," I told her. "What do you think of the name, Christ for Carnies?"

Wendy smiled. "I think it's perfect," she said.

Talk about the blinders being pulled off your eyes! As I walked around with my little family, I started to take real notice of what Wendy and I spoke about. How drawn out and tired these people already looked, and how oblivious those who passed them by really were. It only served to deepen the resolve to help these people and pray for them more.

The kids had a lot of fun that day, and Scott, who took the day off to escort us, got along well with both of my two best friends. My sister and he rode the Ferris Wheel with Rozeanna and me, enabling us to take some beautiful photographs. It felt good, as I had missed doing photography terribly. We got to ride every ride for free, even though I felt a little awkward about it.

"Do you really think, after all you have done, that anyone here is going to say no, you can't ride?" Scott asked me. I smiled a little, and only nodded my head. I didn't do it for a free ride. I did it out of the kindness of my heart. In another way, I felt too, that I was supporting my husband, as a wife is meant to do.

Nightfall came, and I left my kids with Amber, with some money to feed them. However, my friend was upset. Things were going haywire in her life, and I wasn't there. She started to think that I didn't wish to be friends with her, somehow. Never was anything so far from the truth. I just got so involved with helping and caught up with the routine of daily life of a mom of three kids, that I had inadvertently neglected my friends.

Back at WQ, I had Hunter with me, as it was close to his feeding time. I waited patiently for John's boss to keep his promise and release John to spend a few hours with his family. What I got after waiting forty-five minutes was, "You can bring him to lunch for about an hour, and then bring him back. The boy still has work to do. And if he does go with his family, well, he can keep on goin'. " That disheartened both of us. I asked him about his promise, and the man simply shrugged his shoulders and went back to work.

I was on my way back to the carnival, when Amber called, impatient, threatening to put my kids into the van and bring them to my mother's house if I didn't reappear soon. I arrived shortly after, and we erupted into a nasty war of words. I was upset, as was she, and the scene was only broken up by one of the workers, named Andy. I sat and cried, while Andy telephoned John (who now had a cell phone) and told him about the fight. Many of the carnies were concerned as I cried my heart out, and gave me hugs later when I decided to stay at the fair and try not to traumatize the kids anymore than I already had. I wanted to be strong in the eyes of my kids, strong enough to stand during adversity and heartache.

I cemented my resolve to continue the work Christ for Carnies had started.

The days of the fair flew by, and I came out several times with the kids to volunteer. Hunter had a spot on the floor in the food booth, and Rozeanna was just old enough to help hand out sandwiches and cups of soup. Plans were completed to host teardown, for which we acquired a golf cart for distribution. At times I would take a break and walk around the midway, handing out bottles of water that were piled in the bottom of my double stroller and letting Rozeanna enjoy the rides. The grateful workers were smiling, and polite. There was another company joined with us, as often happens with big midways, and they provided water.

"Some companies take care of their workers," a carnie said. "And some don't."

I only nodded and moved on.

Teardown night came soon enough, and I was there for the whole day. The FBC had sent some provisions to add to the other church's supplies. We were in it for the long haul, and a schedule was made out. I had the graveyard shift, from three to eight a.m. We started out with just me, Wendy and the kids.

"God will provide," I told Wendy. "I know he will. We won't be alone in this."

Help arrived around seven o'clock, just an hour before the fair's end, with the arrival of some of Wendy's congregation. We were happy for the three additional people, and had a smooth flow of sandwiches and coffee going strong. I took time out to feed Hunter and put him to sleep, letting Rozeanna help for as long as she could stay awake, reaching over the counter and handing out sandwiches. It warmed everyone's heart when my blue-eyed blonde smiled and said, "God bless you" to everyone she served.

The night grew cold and misty, and Wendy continued to glance out at the cloudy sky. "I hope it doesn't rain," she said softly.

"Because it will delay the teardown?" I asked, spreading peanut butter on a piece of bread.

Wendy shook her head. "No. It will make their job harder to work in the mud."

I stared at Wendy, nearly dropping the knife. "Are you seriously suggesting that they work in the rain? What about a thunder and lightning storm?"

Wendy only shook her head. "The show must go on,"

she said bitterly. "I have seen them in mornings past when we opened the booth. Dehydrated, to the point of falling down. In the rain, it is worse. So many get sick, yet, they keep working until the job is done. If they don't, well, it's the streets for many."

My eyes gravitated to the Big Wheel, just off to the right, and the Ring of Fire, the second tallest ride present, and where John had been assigned to earlier in the week.

"Lord, be with these men and women tonight," I murmured, before going back to work. "Keep them safe."

Around midnight, with Rozeanna fast asleep under a pile of blankets next to her brother in the warmest corner of the booth, the golf cart was loaded for the first run to the far end.

"Not everyone is able to get away, and too many are coming up, trying to grab for their whole crew. Not enough hands," Wendy said. I nodded, and jumped at the chance to take the ride and see this for myself. The kids were safe, Wendy was a good person and a Sister in Christ. She was a mom too, so I felt comfortable letting them stay where they were. In the light drizzle, a young man in his early twenties went with me, leaving his mom with Wendy.

The rides were in various states of tear down, the big wheel lit up, but missing most of its spokes. The Swinger looked as though it was going to tilt off its axis at any moment. We paused for a moment to watch the crew—ten men on each side, pulling out a large spoke from the big wheel. What a process! The tension had to be tight to hold the spoke steady while another man in the center circle loosened the huge bolts with wrenches a little at a time. Despite the cold temperature of about forty degrees, these men were breaking a serious sweat. We didn't want to disturb their concentration and cause an accident, so we waited until the spoke was lowered down by the ropes and lay on the ground, waiting to be put on the truck, before we approached. I realized that I had been holding my breath the entire time.

The supervisor of the wheel saw the golf cart and motioned us over, then turned and called a five minute break to eat. Supplies dwindled quickly as the hungry and grateful men and women at each ride took time out to replenish the enormous energy level needed for this type of job.

We pulled up to the Ring of Fire, the last stop on the first of three runs. The ride looked like a lopsided loop, with one end folded in on itself. There, about half way up, was John, curled like a monkey in a tree, holding on with one hand, attempting to loosen a bolt free with the other. My jaw dropped and my heart slammed in my chest at his precarious position. Then, suddenly, at the call from his boss, he stood up, waving at me. I gave a faltering smile and waved back, watching. John then attempted to push the wrench with his boot, sending it flying through the air and landing a few feet from the man on the ground. It hurt to hear him being cussed out, but I had to bite my tongue as the desire to protect arose. John had done exactly what the man told him to do, yet, he was being screamed at. My partner and I waited until the screamfest was over, and we were finally motioned to approach and distribute.

Our second and third runs went as successfully as the first, and soon we had reached those who needed assistance. The other carnival company that was there took a few sandwiches. Many gave tips, even as we protested, but in the end we decided it would only help in providing for next year's event.

My companions left at 2 a.m., not long after we returned from our run. It was an educational experience I have never forgotten, and gave me a new, healthy respect to how these monster thrill rides are put together and torn apart. Just one miscalculation or mis-calibration, and the sounds of fun could be turned into screams of carnage and death. True, any idiot can push a button, but it takes true smarts, ingenuity and concentration for the rest of the job. A great lesson in "judge not, lest ye be judged," indeed.

That shift I served alone was full of prayer to God, thanking Him for the miracle that we managed to host teardown and provide for this forgotten group of people. A revelation came to me; if our two churches could do it for one fair, what could other churches do to help? I was determined to talk to the Pastor and coordinate with churches in upcoming cities for the rest of the season. Wendy and I had discussed it, but weren't sure how to go about doing it. God, in those silent moments, spoke quietly, as He often does, giving me the answer.

Many of the workers silently came for coffee and cups of soup, and took a sandwich from the basket, letting the tired-out woman slumped in a chair and the two beautiful babies sleep undisturbed in the warmth of the booth.

At the break of dawn, a quiet voice, letting me know that she had taken the last of the coffee, combined with the ache in my back and the stiffness of my knees, reached me across the bridge of sleep. I awoke with a start, and sprang up. A slim, African-American woman wearing a coat two sizes two big for her and a bandana around her head smiled at me and stifled a chuckle.

"I'm sorry, I must have fallen asleep," I said. "Thank you for letting me know. I will make some more coffee right away." I looked a bit distraught that I had slept on duty.

The woman only smiled, sipping her cup. "No worries. We all knew you were asleep, and no one wanted to wake you," the woman replied. "There was enough to last through the night."

I silently wondered how many times the lady came to check the booth, but declined to ask. Instead, I quickly filled the pot with water, put coffee in the filter, and hit the switch for the second urn, the first already gurgling away. A test of the hot water urns proved that there was enough left. Doughnuts would be on the way when the relief team arrived.

The woman quietly watched as I bustled around, making sure that all were provided for.

"Such dedication," she said. "Such sacrifice. It is nice to see. No one has done this much for the carnies. Buying clothes, getting them canned food, ordering all that pizza."

I nodded. "Glad to help," I said softly. "Besides, doesn't it say, 'When you do this for the least of your neighbors, you also do this for me'? Or close to that?" I tried hard to remember seeing her before, but couldn't in that pre-coffee moment.

The woman smiled. "Close to that, yes. Do you think these people are the least in the world?"

I tilted my head. "No," I replied firmly. "Just...forgotten about. I hope to change that."

The woman smiled again. It was the first time I had noticed her eyes, a deep, lovely shade of green, with the light of life present in them. "I believe you will, if you stay true to yourself." She turned to walk away, then turned back. "Remember, it also says, entertain strangers, for unknowingly, you may entertain angels in disguise."

I looked up to reply, and blinked.

Just like that, she was gone.

Wendy was amazed that the booth was still open, thinking I might have shut down to get some shuteye for the night.

"Nope, I told you I was in this for the long haul, and I meant it," I said. Everything was in order, and I had been taking pictures of the dawn between the grey clouds, illuminating the rides as the clouds parted to reveal a spectacular sunrise. It was then I could see how much progress was made, and was amazed how fast the gigantic midway was void of many of the rides in just a short time.

"Well, we have fresh supplies," stated Wendy, who seemed a bit confused. She was certain that we would be much lower on food and the like than we were.

"Loaves and fishes," I said to her, guessing about the look on her face.

"Yes, I guess so," said Wendy happily. "And the doughnuts will help stretch it even more. We can probably go till early afternoon, at least." She sounded pleased, and I nodded.

I told her about the lady that came to visit, and Wendy's eyebrows raised so high they disappeared under her hair.

"Wow, that's interesting," she said. "Maybe she is new?"

"Well, she knew about the pizza," I muttered. "Funny. I thought I knew everyone."

I shrugged it off, and concentrated on the work.

It was then when John came up, covered in grease and smiling, despite the tiredness in his eyes. "We got it done in a good time," he announced, fixing a cup of coffee. "For a first try, anyway. It will go quicker."

"Are you going to sleep now?" I had heard that once the jocks' rides were down, they could go.

John shook his head. "Nope. They need a climber on the Himalaya," he said, pointing to the framework that stood before the cart. "Show Roze and Hunter Daddy at work when they wake up," he asked, blowing me a kiss and walking off, munching on a sandwich.

Where nighttime had offered a glimpse of a world few had seen, daylight brought even more breathtaking and heart-stopping sights. I watched John climb a good sixty-five feet in the air, and lie on his stomach on a ladder inside a small, round portal. His hand reached out, as he yelled, "Jackie, watch this!" and I looked up in time to see him swing in a perfect circle on this tiny ladder. Good thing I have a strong heart, or I would have dropped dead to the ground!

I took a break, watching with my heart in my throat as John turned on his back and rested his hands under his head, waiting for his companions to arrive. I whipped out my camera and snapped off a shot or two. He saw this, and for the next few moments, posed in various positions, waiting for me to signal I had taken the shot. I was actually signaling for him to stop scaring the living heck out of me. But it was something John couldn't understand. I finally whispered thanks to God when Rozeanna woke up and I had to go back inside.

The booth was open until 3 p.m. Monday afternoon, when the last of the food and drink was gone. An hour for clean-up, and the booth was hitched. Happily, no one came up to the booth asking for a last bite or cup of java. I put Hunter and Roze in the carriage and went for a walk once more.

The first fair of the season was over, and the first teardown hosting was a complete success. I stood on the now-barren flatlands of ground as the wind blew sand up and down the rows. I glanced up to God as I wondered what was in store for the future. The next two fairgrounds were a good four hours south, too far for me to drive on a daily basis. The computer and the cell phone I had now would be busy over the next few days. The sun finally burst through about five p.m., when John and Chad and I climbed into the car for the fifteen minute drive back to WQ. One more run and I would bring back Scott and a guy we had gotten to know named Hollywood—nicknamed for the sunglasses he wore.

"You know, Scott," I said as the two climbed into the car. "I would love a carnie nickname."

"Well, many of them are derogatory, you know," he said.

I just shot him a look in the rear view mirror.

"There's just one problem with that," piped up Hollywood. "How do you nickname an angel?"

"Oh, I wouldn't go that far," I said, embarrassed. "Um.... Hey, what about Scout, since I'm going to find other churches to keep hosting you guys?"

The two nodded. "Scout it is," they chorused.

And Scout stuck.

I went home that night, dropping straight into bed beside the kids. Tomorrow would start another day, another phase, another chapter in Christ for Carnies, which would become much, much more involved than I ever dreamed.

Christ for Carnies

— 4 —

The Mission

By Wednesday that week, the train rolled out to begin the season of '09. I was there with the kids to give them a quiet sendoff, my husband standing on the steps of the train waving and blowing kisses. The kids' interest was caught, in awe of the blue and white cars with their colorful flags waving in the breeze, and the rides, in various strange shapes and sizes. All too soon, the train rolled out of sight, blending with the sun as it traveled west to switch tracks to the South. I was left with nothing but the silence of the wind once more.

I turned back to the car and went home. The Pastor was busy compiling a list for me, and I started making phone calls the following day. It was a bit disappointing, however. I called other churches and found some willing to help; some said they only helped their own. I wondered what "their own" really meant. Weren't we all Children of God? And I even asked that question of one priest. I was stunned by the reply.

"All except drug users and carnies," he said.

I made a note to never set foot in that place, and to start praying for an end to that way of thinking.

A friendly voice was heard a week later, however, when the sister church of Fort Pierce answered, and promised help. Help, though, came with one request.

"Would you mind terribly coming down this Sunday and addressing the congregation in person?" I told them I would try.

I thought about this seriously. There were many things to consider, such as the long drive for one. The other thing was, where to stay? If I were going to go, it have to be for a few days. To drive back and forth that distance in one day was ludicrous. I lifted my eyes to the Lord.

"What do I do?" I asked.

The answer came in a form I did not expect, and certainly was not to my liking. However, the Lord allows things to happen for His plan and purpose, even though we don't understand.

An argument broke out between me and my parents, because they weren't happy with how things were working out at this time. They thought, since I had some money, I should be in my own apartment.

"How would I keep it?" I asked. Sure, the money in the bank would last me a little while, but what happened when it ran out? Jobs were scarce already, with no signs of improvement in sight. I would be moving right back into their house, or a shelter, when it came to an end. Opinions were aired, and we all left the house in frustration for different destinations. My parents went for a mini vacation to the Keys, and I headed for Ft. Pierce.

"God will provide," I whispered, heading south.

I didn't let John know I was coming, I just suddenly

appeared, much to his, and many other people's delight. I made a stop just before appearing, and soon had the bottom of the stroller full of water once more. It is how I decided we would let everyone know that we had come for a visit. The weather was warm now, a glaring sun in a cloudless sky and a rogue wind from the coast made for rough conditions. Sunblock was handed out with the water; though they were the trial size bottles, the guys and gals were happy for it. Rozeanna was thrilled we were at the carnival again, and enjoyed her favorite rides.

I didn't make it a habit to hover around John's ride, which was the Ring of Fire. In fact, I made it a point to glance down and judge the crowd before even approaching the gate that surrounded it. If there were a long line, I would go the other way, or around it, as best I could. If there were no one around, I would approach, give him and his co-worker their water, get a kiss for myself and one for the kids, and then keep going. I wanted to make it clear I wasn't a pesky spouse.

Night fell, and the dilemma became clear—I did not have a place to stay yet for the night. Feigning tiredness, I drove John over to the train, which was parked on the tracks around two miles from the gate near the coast. The men of Car Seven decided I was not going to be sleeping in my car and arranged for me to sleep on the train, provided I was off before roll call at eight AM. I nodded— it was no problem. I had to sleep on my side, with Rozeanna facing me. Hunter lay over my head lengthwise in the small alcove, blocked in so he could not fall out. John slept on the top bunk.

The next day was more of the same: passing out water stored in the bottom of my double stroller, letting Roze go on rides. It was not easy to do, since the entire midway was in the dirt, and this fair was huge. Much of the day was spent in the picnic table pavilion, where Rozeanna could run around inside when it wasn't horribly crowded, and Hunter could roll around on a large blanket. It was a covered with a wooden roof, so we were in the shade, and fans kept us nice and cool. I took this opportunity to make phone calls for the next stop in Vero Beach, and make contact with the church pastors, as well as the Salvation Army, who would become a real godsend in the next few days. The stroller reclined, so it was easy to give both children a nap after lunch, which I carried in my backpack. Sometimes it would be a can of soup or a can of beans. Always, it was something nutritious and non-perishable.

The pavilion came with a special bonus, as it happened to be between the Ring of Fire and the Gravitron, and across from the rollercoaster. Behind us, we were blocked in by the bumper cars. All these were run by the friends we had made, and I felt it was God's will that it happened that way. They could watch out for us, while we watched out for them. I was happy, too; it was next to the Ring of Fire. For the supervisors who watched me silently, making sure I wasn't doing something illegal, they instead saw a dedicated spouse showing her daughter what daddy did for work, and a helpful soul to the others. They also saw that we did not make pests of ourselves, and occupied our time well. I read the Bible and other books to the kids. It didn't matter that Hunter just looked at me with a silly grin and Rozeanna was running around playing. What matters is that they heard what I read. Rear a child from the beginning the right way, and he will continue to follow the right path as an adult.

I wondered if Rozeanna was learning a lesson or two from all of this in the art of giving. I wondered too, if Hunter was absorbing anything. Never once did I question if this was right—the way things were going, with all the connections made and the eager voices on the other line to jump in and help, I knew that it was God's will. I was determined to take it as far as it would go.

Sunday dawned bright and clear once more, and I escaped the train again long before roll call. I had a mission today, and would join the carnival later. Today, I was going to address the Missionary Alliance and the Salvation Army in the area, making my case for Christ for Carnies. It was teardown night, so there was not much time to get things together, and I silently wondered if it would fly at all. But I am not a person to give up. Armed with pictures of the previous teardown, I pulled up to the congregation. I had stopped at a rest area to wash up and dress the kids. As was the case with our church, everyone fell in love with Roze and Hunter, and I truly think that once the congregation learned that their daddy was among the men and women they were about to help, God strengthened the desire to be of assistance in their hearts.

Through the sermon, I wondered what the heck to say. I had no pre-set speech, had no rehearsed words to give to these folks. Just a handful of pictures, and what I felt in my heart.

As God would have it, the pastor chose a wonderful sermon on helping others and reaching beyond the church walls. Whether he chose it in the event of my arrival for the mission or it was coincidence doesn't matter—it only showed that I wasted my time worrying, for the Lord's plan was in effect, and things would fall in place.

The pastor read from Isaiah, paragraph, 58, verses 6, 7 and 10.

"Is not this the kind of fasting I have chosen: to lose the chains of injustice and untie the cords of the yoke, to set the oppressed free and break every yoke? Is it not to share your food with the hungry and to provide the poor wanderer with shelter-- when you see the naked, to clothe him, and not to turn away from your own flesh and blood? ...and if you spend yourselves in behalf of the hungry and satisfy the needs of the oppressed, then your light will rise in the darkness, and your night will become like the noonday."

This passage struck home with me. I felt that it was the Lord was speaking to me, and not a pastor preaching a sermon. I felt it was a message for me not to worry; that recent events and the events to come were all part of the plan somehow, and somehow, everything would be OK, as long as I held on to my faith. I straightened up and listened more closely, borrowing from the lesson to form my own words.

"In 1 John, verse 3, 17-18, it says: If anyone has material possessions and sees his brother in need but has no pity on him, how can the love of God be in him? Dear children, let us not love with words or tongue but with actions and in truth. And on that note, I would like to introduce to you a member from the Faith Baptist Church north of us. She is here on behalf of a mission called Christ for Carnies."

I got up, followed by Rozeanna, who was helping me to wheel the stroller with Hunter, now fast asleep, to the front.

"Good afternoon, everyone," I began. "Thank you for having us here today to your lovely church, and for allowing me to speak." I paused a moment, to start passing out the pictures I had. "I took these pictures on the first tear-

The Mission

down night, just a few weeks ago. I have a few video clips," I said, passing my camera around and showing how to make it play.

"My husband joined the carnival in mid-January, because, well, roofing is pretty much gone in this state, just like construction." Many nodded their heads. "It broke my heart, because that night, the first night of that cold snap we had? He used an electric grill to produce heat so he wouldn't freeze. He was one of the lucky ones—many others didn't even have sheets on the bed. With the aid of God, my pastor and I called a few places, and got hold of enough blankets, sheets, towels, pillows and cases for every worker, and we handed them out that night." I stopped, as people applauded, and I turned red.

"Well, we also got food and other supplies for them. That's how Christ for Carnies was started. Now, has anyone seen, or know about, teardown? When they take down the rides?"

"I know that they're gone pretty quickly," said one parishioner.

"Yes. That is because, after working all day at the fair, like today, they will begin taking the rides down as soon as the fair is over and people are leaving." I paused, to meet the eyes of every person in the room for effect. "That means, they started working at 8 a.m. this morning, to maintain the rides, and will not stop, no break, until tomorrow afternoon around four or five."

Everyone grew quiet, and some were even looking at their watches. I nodded my head.

"Your pastor was kind enough to ask me to speak to you all about this. The items we need are simple. Cans of coffee, tea bags, water bottles. cup of soup, bread, peanut butter and jelly. Oh, and cups, napkins and spoons, sugar and creamer. Enough to last through the night."

Murmurs went through the crowd now. A gentleman raised his hand.

"So, you're not after money?" He asked. "I mean, it's not that kind of donation? A lot of people hesitate because, well, a lot of carnies are criminal, and take advantage."

I nodded. "Sure, some *are* criminal. But, does that necessarily mean that they should be forgotten? Or helped? Some are trying to move on, forget their past. Others, well...." I motioned to my kids. "Their father is one, as I previously said. And does that mean that those who are like my husband should be excluded from help?"

Many shook their heads. I was forever grateful for the pastor as he stood up and quoted another passage from the Bible at that point.

"In Matthew 25, verse 41 to 45, it says, 'Then he will say to those on his left, "Depart from me, you who are cursed, into the eternal fire prepared for the devil and his angels. For I was hungry and you gave me nothing to eat, I was thirsty and you gave me nothing to drink, I was a stranger and you did not invite me in, I needed clothes and you did not clothe me, I was sick and in prison and you did not look after me." They also will answer, "Lord, when did we see you hungry or thirsty or a stranger or needing clothes or sick or in prison, and did not help you?" He will reply, "I tell you the truth, whatever you did not do for one of the least among you, you did not do for me."'"

Another pause, and I again met the eyes of the people in the congregation. I could see them weighing the words in their mind.

"The smallest kindness goes a long way."

One woman raised her hand. "I will be happy to go and get some supplies," she said. I smiled and thanked her. A few more murmured that they too, would join the lady in getting supplies, and would have them here for me to pick up at six o'clock. I didn't know what to expect, but I was happy for anything, and would make it last as long as I could.

In the meantime, a woman kindly asked me to follow her to the store nearby, so she could load me up with some water to distribute.

"It's really humid out there, " she said. "Maybe they would appreciate some of it now."

I smiled and nodded, and thanked the pastor for his support. He told me that Pastor Ron had also called him with information, stating the mission had FBC's full support. I smiled brightly then. Good ol' Pastor Ron…I would have to thank him for that.

The lady I followed packed my car to the roof with water, and for a moment I feared I might not have room for whatever the church was going to give at six. But again I should not have worried, because I found the main supervisor and explained the situation to him. He was very kind about it, and liked the idea, remembering what we had done a few weeks before. I was able to put the water under the table they conjured up at the place I was going to use.

When I looked the table over, I realized there was a problem. What would I use to make coffee and hot water in? An inquiry to a few of the guys and gals themselves provided a quick answer, when four people entrusted me with their precious coffee pots. I wondered then about how silly it seemed, to be possessive of such an item.

Six o'clock rolled around, and I was right on time. My heart leaped and tears sprang as I saw the items spread out before me. There was plenty enough to go all night, all right, and supplies enough to go on to the next spot, too! That was good; I hadn't been able to reach the Pastor of the Alliance there. All part of God's plan, I thought.

Packed and loaded, I drove back to the fair, after feeding the kids their fellowship dinner, and then waited for the fair to close. The kids were sleeping, so I pushed the driver's seat back a little and took a nap, too.

I woke up to a sharp rap on the window. There was Chad, who happened to be passing by and saw us. I smiled at him and nodded.

"You all right?" he asked quietly.

"Yes, we were just waiting till the fair ended, so I can set up," I told him.

"Oh. Fair ends in twenty minutes," He said. "Good thing I passed by." He grinned. "You were snoring away."

"Oh…geez…" I said, embarrassed. "Thanks for letting me know. I have to get the car up toward the Sling Shot. Any paths that lead there?"

"Yeah. Go around the Bobs, and hook a sharp left. In fact, give me about ten minutes or so after the fair closes, and I'll let you in."

I nodded, and waited.

True to his word, Chad let me in, and I drove slowly toward the spot. The kids were still asleep, which was good. I started unloading the car, and set up. It took me almost an hour before the coffee pots started perking, hot water started steaming, and the first sandwiches were made and covered.

Soon, there was a line of men and the few ladies wanting something to eat. I manned the station for the next three hours, and luckily, the kids slept through the night.

I fell asleep around two o'clock, when the mad rush had ebbed and no one had been seen for half an hour. I made sure that the coffee and water urns were full, and there were sandwiches made, hidden under a donated screen tent. I headed for the driver's seat again, and snoozed. There was a sign on the table, *PLEASE WAKE ME WHEN THE COFFEE OR WATER LOOKS LOW.* No one woke me, but I slept so lightly that I knew when a person would tip-toe by.

It was around 6:30 a.m. when the sun began to part the curtain of darkness, and its fingers of light tickled opened my eyelids. I hung a small blanket on the two hooks behind the front seats so it would not wake up the children, and set about making more coffee. I was astonished, though—a fresh pot had already been made, and I wondered which kind soul had done so, rather than wake me up. The sandwiches were gone, however, so I started making some.

A man approached a few minutes later, and I gave him a greeting. But his manner of dress and the disapproving look on his face had me wondering if he was a carnie at all.

"I just came over to see what the fuss was about," he growled.

"Fuss?" I asked.

"Yeah, fuss," the man repeated. He then pointed a finger at me. "You are cutting into my business."

"I beg your pardon?" I asked.

"As I said. YOU are cutting into my business with this. How much are you charging?"

"Ah...this is free," I replied. "It's a love offering from the church."

"Yeah, well, see, in this spot, I stay open all night for these guys. You see, the way I see it, is this." The man grew closer. "These guys are the dregs of society, yet they somehow managed to get this job, and get a paycheck. I'm here, to get as much of their check as possible."

I really didn't know what to say at first, and just blinked.

The man took my quietness as a sign of intimidation, and drew closer, reaching out to curl his fist around the collar of my jacket.

"I suggest you cut and run while you still can," he snarled.

I was calm, and slowly grabbed the pot of hot water, looking him straight into the eye.

"Judge not, least ye be judged," I said quietly, my hand curling tight around the pot, which was full. "And not all the people that work here are 'dregs.' My husband does it to support his family. I am here, to support them, and him." A deep breath, then exhale.... "I suggest, sir, you get your hands off of me."

"Or you will do what?" he asked, raising his hand.

I threw the scalding hot water toward his face. He let go quickly, and tripped over a crack in the sidewalk, screaming obscenities that would make a sailor blush. I ran from behind the table, the pot of coffee now in the other hand, and advanced toward him. I was only going to use it if I needed to.

The man stood up, facing me. His fist was clenched, his lips twisted in anger. "You're through here, goody two-shoes," he hissed. But when he saw the pot of coffee in my hands he backed up a little. "Wait until the fair commissioner hears about this."

"The fair commissioner is the one who gave me the permission to be here," I told him calmly, standing now between the front door of the car and the table. "I think it is a shame. But I am asking you sir, to leave, and not to ever touch me in any manner again."

The man growled, and promised to get me thrown off the property as he walked away. I waited until he was out of sight, and put the coffee pot down, then sank to my knees. I gave thanks then and there to God that nothing more serious had happened—the water I threw largely missed him. I was shaking. I didn't know what the man was really going to do. It never occurred to me that there would be danger during a mission at a carnival in the USA.

When the fair commissioner came over, it was the man who threatened me who was told to pack up his store, and not return.

Justice was served...and I was happy, in a way. At least for this fairground, no one would be gouging people's hard-earned pay. I told my husband, Chad, Scott and a few others about it. They applauded my bravery but told me that I should have screamed for help.

"Don't you know, that any of us would defend you, little sis?" asked Will, another worker who had a fondness for me as the sister he never had. "You ever have any problems, you let us know."

I promised to do just that.

The kids woke up, and I gave Roze a peanut butter and jelly sandwich for breakfast. On a patch of grass I made a makeshift tent between the car door and a metal stick that held a sign at one time. I also put a blanket on the ground so Hunter could roll around, and made sure there were no red ant hills nearby. I fed him, thankful that breast feeding was successful for him, as it wasn't for Rozeanna or Joe.

My supplies started dwindling around noon, and I was completely out of bread and peanut butter by two. Sugar and creamer ran out around that time, and the coffee had to be drunk black. There was little demand for it now, since people wanted the water instead. It was 3:45 when the water ran out, and I started packing up. It was OK, because John arrived a half hour later, just as I put the last of the stuff inside the car. But I still had some coffee pots to return.

While returning the last coffee pot, I nearly tripped over Chad. He was asleep on the ground, just under the bunkhouse in the cool shade. His eyes barely opened, just widely enough to see who had disturbed him.

"I'm sorry, I whispered. "Just returning the coffee pot."

He nodded, and went back to sleep, muttering that he only had a four-hour nap. Chuck was part of the roller-coaster crew, and that was a three day teardown job.

I drove John back from the fairgrounds to the train, and had to snap a picture of him. He was so exhausted; he couldn't even sit up straight. There was so much stuff behind the seat; he couldn't lean back, so he ended up leaning over a coffee pot, a water urn, and some clothes. The look on his worn face—I took a picture of him that way, to remind myself later how much this man loved his family, and how hard he fought to never give up. It also amazed me how he held fast to his Faith without worrying as much as I did.

It broke my heart to wake him up a few minutes later to tell him he was at the train. He was so tired that he resembled a drunken man with no control over his movements going up the steps of the train to his bed. My heart leaped out to him.

- 5 -
Vero Beach

Vero Beach, only twenty miles north, was next on the list, and it was one site that concerned me. John was a bit surprised when I followed the train. I told him it was only twenty miles north of Ft. Pierce, and I had a meeting with the Salvation Army in the area. Both were true, but I hid from him the fact that I had left my parents' house because of an argument, and couldn't go back until things cooled off. He was hoping I would go home, and be safe.

Things had changed a lot in the carnival world, and even if we were with him, we still couldn't live on the train. Once meant for families, and so pretty on the outside, the eighty-plus-year-old train was actually very dilapidated, with peeling paint (and possibly lead), sagging ceilings and holes in the floor. Not to mention the infestation of spiders, roaches and more. The men had to spray their bunks every so often. The bunk houses were a lot cleaner because they were newer, but they were less than half the size.

I did not hesitate to contact the Salvation Army and find the nearest store. A bonus was that only a half mile down the road was a thrift shop run by the Baptist Church. It was chock full of items the guys had been looking for, and at reasonable prices. Not too much further up the road was a host of fast food and dine-in restaurants. The farthest up the road was the big chain store everyone frequented. Because of the distance, the guys would "tip" me five dollars for a ride.

I met with the Captain of the Salvation Army later that afternoon, armed with the same handful of pictures I had at the church, the Pastor's phone number and the same speech.

"That's incredible," said the Captain, sitting back in his chair. "In all the years the fair has been around, I never thought about it. Thank you for bringing their plight to light." He smiled at me, shaking my hand. "I will meet tonight with the team, and we will discuss what we will do. We are on board," he assured me. "And tell your husband he is doing an incredible job."

"I will," I said to him. "Thank you."

"We will be in touch soon," the Captain said. "I will call your cell phone."

I nodded, and left, ready to distribute water once more.

The dirt on the midway turned to mud after a good rainstorm. Rides sat in various stages of setup during the week, and I ran people off to the various stores, eateries and businesses. A few I drove to the bus stop, one, unhappily, to the highway—his plan was to hitchhike home. I said a prayer with him for a safe journey. It would be months later before I found out that he had arrived, and was doing fine. But for the moment, I put him in God's hands.

Another part of the mission was going to the various churches, finding food banks and the like that would be so kind as to donate some canned goods. I helped when I could, stocking the car, and yes, now our bunkhouse as well, as fully as I could. It was well-known that anyone could come to my "house" and eat. John and the others figured out that I was there to stay for a while, eventually coaxing me to talk about the altercation with my parents, and the hurt feelings I harbored. I realized later I was using the ministry to get away from those feelings, something *good* to focus on in an effort to overcome the negativity. But I felt needed and respected, which made me happy. Somehow, this tiny ministry was making a big difference.

We traveled with two other companies that operated various rides. All of their carnies knew that I wasn't a "lot lizard," a single woman with or without children who follows the carnivals and making her living by the oldest profession in the book. Many called me "Miss Jackie." Most called me "Ma'm' while tipping their baseball caps, and those who knew me best called me Scout or Angel. The latter would always make me blush and give them a playful swipe. I would tell them I wasn't perfect, and it was a team effort, never just me. Yes, I was doing the majority of the ground work. But if it weren't for the Lord's moving hearts and the Pastor's answering the incessant calls asking just who I was and was this for real, Christ for Carnies wouldn't have stood a chance.

The bunkhouse the kids and I slept in was very small. Around ten feet tall by eight feet long, this particular bunk was only four feet wide. You could also describe it as a bed in a box with shelves on each wall. That was it. But all we did was sleep in it. I slept on my side, terrified of falling off, and keeping an eye on the blanket we had for a door. Yes, a blanket—that room had been in a slight accident, where the door was sheared off. Will and Blaze, who had the head bunks on each side and were very good friends, made it absolutely clear that any person who dared to infiltrate my room would get a beating. The two of them were known to keep their word. Only one person dared to make the attempt. The fight outside woke me, and I jumped out of the bed to peek through the curtain. Every guy in the other nine bunks was outside, joined by a few others that bordered me, to "take out the trash." I got a quick apology for being disturbed, and was asked politely to go back to bed. I do not know who it was or what happened to that person, and could only pray for him. I had been told that the kids and I were family, and family watched out for each other.

The rides also came to an end after I had to throw a man out of the car, single-handedly, when he made me a proposition. I had three rules in my car that were to be strictly obeyed. One—no smoking in my car, period. I am allergic to smoke, and my kids don't need it in their lungs. My mom was slowly dying from its effects; I didn't need it around me any more. Second rule—no drugs—not in your pockets, not on your person. I was *not* to be used as a drug runner or I would call the police myself. Three? I was married, so don't ask. After the third man was thrown out for breaking these rules, the rides halted, except for a select few people that I had come to know from the beginning, or for someone approved by my newfound brothers. It wasn't that anyone wanted to curb the mission, it was for our safety.

Arrangements were being made by the management to bring John off the train and into the bunkhouse, but that wouldn't happen till the end of the fair. In the meantime,

I continued to walk the midway at certain times, handing out water. At night, I would start distributing any canned goods that I found, or bought from gift certificates I received, donated by different stores. The letters from the church were a godsend in getting this done. I also started offering to do laundry, since there was a laundry truck on site, or I would go to the laundromat down the road.

Then it was time for the kids to play, and a visit to the beach was also on the schedule. The beach was not so far away, and at times I made early morning runs, bringing my "family" members there. Some of them needed the peace and quiet, others had never seen the beach before in their lives. The powers that be in management actually surprised everyone with a trip to the beach one day, and the few hours rest and relaxation was an enjoyment. John, the kids and I joined them, and it warmed my heart to see John make connections with his children, especially Hunter, who was only five months old.

A blessing came on the first Saturday of the fair, when I received the phone call I was waiting for from the Salvation Army. I held my breath at first, and exhaled with a smile as they told me that they would be happy to come out with a truck on both Sundays and feed the workers. They would not, however, be able to host teardown that night. I thanked them, grateful that at least there would be one good, wholesome meal for everyone, for free.

True to their word, they came at four o'clock, and had enough food to feed around five hundred people. I happily loaded my stroller with water, and pushed through the mud (it had rained overnight) to follow the food cart. The joinees (people who run the stands) looked a bit suspicious at first, but they were happy to have one free meal. Some declined, stating they had enough, and asked me to give their shares give to those who didn't. The rest were grateful and really smiling. Some even whispered, "God bless you," for the first time in years.

A bagpipe player strolled through, and for a moment, I thought of my grandpa. He was a tall, redheaded Irishman, and stubborn to the core. I felt as though he were passing me by, smiling, approving what we were doing. That made me smile for the first time in a week. I had called and made contact with my mom and dad, and we did talk, but I could tell the tension was still there. I decided to wait a little bit. In some ways, I wanted to go back to that one room in my parents' house the four of us had shared. It seemed a lot roomier now after staying in the bunkhouse. Maybe that was the point for me—to learn to be happy with what you have. I clung to that as I distributed the bottles of water.

A Fair Commissioner came by to congratulate us and thank the Salvation Army for doing something so very kind. The Captain in charge pointed to me and said, "Thank this lady for alerting us to the need."

I blushed from the praise and waved it off. I was only doing what I thought anyone else could do.

Life in the carnie world is not so vastly different from what everyone considers "civilized" and "respectful." It amazed truly me to think how many times I drove by a carnival as a teenager, laughing a little at the workers, and wondering how anyone could really live this lifestyle. I was receiving my comeuppance there, I supposed. After the fair would end for the night, everyone would tiredly return to their bunks. If laundry needed to be done, they did it. Most of them smoke and drank, talking about their hard day of keeping people safe. Just as office workers gather around the water cooler, these men and women also talked about the day's mishaps and events, cracked a joke or two, and got a good laugh out of the antics of the customers on their ride. Quite a few would visit another, and many shared their fire or their stew. That Tuesday night as we all dumped a can of something into the pot reminded me of the lesson about sharing that Mrs. Connie gave at the Ladies Bible Study. We all came dressed as hobos, and picked names from a hat, (Hunter's Hobo name was Stinky Soggybottom…no lie!) and shared what's known as "Hobo Soup," which was exactly what we were preparing this night. Here were these folks, misunderstood, judged, and poor, sharing what they had from the heart, to make sure no one went hungry.

A full moon in the sky gave me the opportunity for photographs I would otherwise not have been able to capture. I took rare shot of the big wheel by the moonlight, plus several wonderful night shots of different rides in full swing.

John came the next day to the bunkhouse to stay. Four of us in that tiny box was a little rough, but I didn't care. We were together once again, and that's what was important. The bed for the lower bunk was roomy enough for John and, with Rozeanna above our heads and Hunter in a makeshift crib on the floor by our heads. This bunkhouse also had a locking door and a working window with a screen for air. Much better than a blanket for a door!

The days flew by, and teardown was upon us. The Salvation Army came out again, this time around 7 p.m. They wanted to feed the workers a hearty meal of beef stew, potatoes and a mix of vegetables as close to closing as they could, and gave each person two extra bottles of water for the night to come.

I worried terribly once more. I had not been able to contact the pastor of the Alliance church in the area. A phone call to Pastor Ron finally gave me the reason why—through his channels, he found that the pastor had taken his family on vacation. If only I had known that sooner! I finished helping the Salvation Army and shot off to the nearest grocery store, a good half hour away, buying the supplies for the night myself.

This teardown night, however, was anything but normal. I was caught up in a long line of traffic, and stopped by a police officer at a sobriety road check area. Of course, I had nothing but two kids, coffee, tea, and cup-of-soups. While I waited for them to check my license, I asked the officer what he thought of the carnies.

"Some are decent," the officer replied. "Some...leave a lot to be desired. It's a job I couldn't do, that's for sure," he added.

I was finally let go, thanks to a clean record, and sent on my way. More traffic, as I wondered what the hold-up was about. I never did find out, as the line of cars winded past the carnival, where I needed to turn off.

A flash of jagged lightning forked across the sky as I started making my way down the dirt road to the bunk house. Thunderstorms are nothing to fool around with, period, especially in Florida. I held my breath as I counted and only got to three before thunder rolled across the night. A glance towards the rides showed some going in full swing. I sent up a silent prayer that the rain would hold off till tomorrow.

But it wasn't meant to be.

As soon as I pulled up in between the bunk houses and threw the car into park, the skies opened and buckets of water came pouring down, signaling the end of the fair for Vero Beach.

I sat, stunned. The supplies would be limited, of course. But where was I going to set up, out of the rain? What about the kids? I had planned on setting up in the same pavilion that the Salvation Army had used, letting the kids sleep in the car. I couldn't do that in this maelstrom! I took out my camera and videotaped a portion of everyone working in this crazy weather, as the big wheel behind me spun and people walked around as though the sun were shining.

A rap on the window startled me, and Blaze, the security guard, jumped into the car for a moment.

"Look, I know you give us food 'n' such for teardown. But none of us want you and those kids out in this." He gave me a pointed look. "Got it? Get them kids in your house, and keep them and yourself warm. All of us will manage just fine."

I nodded, and I know he could see the disappointment in my face. "Don't worry," he told me. "we all have done this before. Like I said, we don't want you and them babies out. And if you do, well, your brothers will give you a whoopin'."

He got out of the car to help. I grabbed Rozeanna, who was behind me, and he grabbed Hunter. I ran the five feet to the door, unlocked it, and jumped in. Blaze had covered Hunter's seat with his jacket. The kids were in, and lay on the bed covered up.

"I'm still making coffee," I insisted. "There is water in the trunk, and the soup. I can—"

"NO." His words were firm. "NO one is to come to your bunk. No one but your husband, and your bunkmates. If you don't recognize anyone, don't open this door. Got me?"

I knew better than to argue, and merely nodded. "Got it."

No sooner was the coffee made then John came bounding into the bunk, soaked to the bone and shivering.

"Oh good, coffee," he said, giving me a kiss. A glance at the bed, and he leaned over to kiss the kids' cheeks. "Don't open this door—"

"Unless I recognize the person from the show. I know," I told him, wondering if there was something more going on to warrant that kind of warning.

John nodded, filled his travel mug, and hurried out the door.

I thought this was a good time to read the Bible. It was going to be a long, long night for everyone, as the wind kicked up and the storm raged.

I decided to read Mark 4, verses 35-41, about Jesus calming the storm.

"That day when evening came, He said to His disciples, 'Let us go over to the other side.' Leaving the crowd behind, they took him along, just as he was, in the boat. There were also other boats with him. A furious squall came up, and the waves broke over the boat, so that it was nearly swamped. Jesus was in the stern, sleeping on a cushion. The disciples woke him and said to him, 'Teacher, don't you care if we drown?'

He got up, rebuked the wind and said to the waves, 'Quiet! Be still!' Then the wind died down and it was completely calm.

He said to his disciples, 'Why are you so afraid? Do you still have no faith?'

They were terrified and asked each other, 'Who is this? Even the wind and the waves obey him!'"

I glanced out the window. "Lord, please calm the storm," I whispered.

I kept reading, choosing Acts 27, verses 13-26, also about a storm.

"When a gentle south wind began to blow, they thought they had obtained what they wanted; so they weighed anchor and sailed along the shore of Crete. Before very long, a wind of hurricane force, called the 'northeaster,' swept down from the island. The ship was caught by the storm and could not head into the wind; so we gave way to it and were driven along. As we passed to the lee of a small island called Cauda, we were hardly able to make the lifeboat secure. When the men had hoisted it aboard, they passed ropes under the ship itself to hold it together. Fearing that they would run aground on the sandbars of Syrtis, they lowered the sea anchor and let the ship be driven along. We took such a violent battering from the storm that the next day they began to throw the cargo overboard. On the third day, they threw the ship's tackle overboard with their own hands. When neither sun nor stars appeared for many days and the storm continued raging, we finally gave up all hope of being saved.

After the men had gone a long time without food, Paul stood up before them and said: 'Men, you should have taken my advice not to sail from Crete; then you would have spared yourselves this damage and loss. But now I urge you to keep up your courage, because not one of you will be lost; only the ship will be destroyed. Last night an angel of the God whose I am and whom I serve stood beside me and said, "Do not be afraid, Paul. You must stand trial before Caesar; and God has graciously given you the lives of all who sail with you." So keep up your courage, men, for

I have faith in God that it will happen just as he told me. Nevertheless, we must run aground on some island.'"

I was mulling over these two passages for a while, comparing them to the storms of adversity we had been through in our life. My mom was a perfect example, for all the years of health issues and heartaches she had been through.

A sharp wrap at the door woke me up, and the Bible fell to the floor as I stood.

"Jackie, it's me," said John, and I immediately unlocked the door.

He stepped in, water squishing out of his boots. I was instantly alarmed—it was only two o'clock. I knew that the Ring of Fire would take longer than that.

"I told T.J. that I was going to the bathroom," he quickly explained, pouring himself more coffee and taking a sip. "He's out there screaming at me to move faster. On slippery steel, no less."

John sat on the bed, removing his boots.

"Find me some dry clothes, please?" he pleaded.

I dragged the suitcase from under the bed and popped it open, grabbing the clothes he would need.

"I have never worked so hard, Jackie," John said. I just kneeled and started helping to take off John's wet clothes, drying his skin with a towel. "And he's out there screaming at me. Not in this crap. I am *not* going to kill myself. I'm going to take my time."

"You'd better not kill yourself," I growled, half playful, half serious, as I put on his dry socks. "We need you."

John leaned over to give me a long kiss. "I need you, all of you too," he whispered.

Another cup of coffee after he finished dressing, and out the door he went.

This ritual happened three times during the night, though the last time was to get John in his pajamas and into bed. The sky, still pouring, turned a lighter grey. Normally, John would be out there, helping others...but not today. And let T.J. or anyone else come to that door and wake him, and they would have to deal with an angry and upset wife.

There was no room on the bed, so sprawled out were John and the kids, so I threw a couple of blankets on the floor, folded a jacket for a pillow, and fell asleep.

No one else came to the door. Bunkhouses were taken out starting at dawn, but we were one of the last bunkhouses to go out, a day and a half later. I was glad for the break. Everyone was. It was the first time they got a full day of sleep after teardown, and everyone kind of kept to themselves. John and I went up to the store with the kids, picking up a tent. We decided, since it was warm outside, we were going to camp for a while, and relieve the crowding in the bunkhouse. Pizza was ordered, and our bunk family had a small private party.

Around ten the next day our bunk house was picked up, and we went to Winter Quarters once more, setting up the tent just outside the bunkhouse door. The tent offered many options, including a safe, cool place for the kids to play during the day while I watched over them. I also did laundry for several people, while John went with the crew to set up for the next spot in Sanford, Florida...part of my old stomping grounds as a kid.

– 6 –
Seminole County Fair

Sanford at one time was largely an older downtown section, surrounded by cow pastures and a few businesses near the highway, offering things to eat, sleep, and gas for the weary traveler. That all changed in the 90s, when the sleepy cow town erupted into a commercial blitz. A main mall, several strip malls surrounding it, tons of restaurants from drive-through to fancy dine in, movie theaters and more. At the southwest corner of the mall a dirt road used to bring you into the woods, one of many teenage hideouts. I sat with my best friend Ginger in a '69 fastback Mustang, picking out cars coming off the bridge, grabbing the CB and teasing all truckers within range. Ah, the good old days.

I gave that corner a grinning salute as I rounded the now-normal road that went to the back entrance of the mall, where the Seminole County Fair was being set up.

It had been a favorite haunt this time of the year, especially for us that lived right over the bridge. Those ghosts of the teenage and young adult yesteryears floated in my mind as I got the kids out of the car and started the rations of water once more.

Our church, the FBC, would be hosting the end of this fair and I couldn't have been happier. The congregation was excited at this new outreach, and I had been to church since our return from Vero Beach to tell about the success down south. I also expressed my concerns about the storms, and how my heart hammered in my chest, worried about John's six-foot four-inch frame standing on that slippery steel circle, eighty-five feet in the air. Many reassured me that God had to have been with him, for lightning to avoid that kind of beacon.

I had begun to talks had begun with my parents, a good sign things were calming down. I hoped that I had shown that I stood by my husband, stood to honor my vows said in church. Isn't that how I was raised? On the other hand, I did understand my parent's concern, and I appreciated the fact that they cared enough to raise a fuss about it. My mom and I butted heads often, because we were too much alike, I think. My parents' health worried me greatly, mom's especially. Not only had she said things like, "That is it, all my grandchildren," when Hunter was born, but in January, I had a dream come true—one of my pictures had been chosen for an Artist Reception in the Sanford Welcome Center, just down the road from where I now stood. Mom and Dad went to the reception, something that left me overjoyed. In a whispered moment, however, my mom kissed my cheek, telling me that now she didn't have to be here to know that one day I would succeed. I told mom, half jokingly, that she had to stick around, there would be more to come, to which she replied, "It doesn't matter—I was here for the first."

I also left messages on Amber's voice mail. I missed her terribly, and wanted my friend back, to do things right. I had a lot of time to think about it, and saw where I went wrong. I was hoping, for the sake of our friendship, that the issue could be resolved.

My mom's words and others had played in my heart over and over recently, and I silently wondered if it was a message from God. But for now, I had water to give out.

"Hey, Jackie," called Chad, seeing me cross the grounds. "Can you do me a favor? We can't go into the mall, and —"

"Huh?" I interrupted. "What do you mean, you can't go into the mall?"

"Well, management doesn't really want us in there," Chad told me. "We're carnies. A while back, a few people got caught stealing. Ruined it for the rest of us."

"Wha...what?" I glanced over to the building at the shoulder. Not go into the mall, because they were carnies? Incredible.

"What do you want me to get?" I asked. Chad just grinned. By now he knew the look on my face, and that I was plenty upset and about to do something about it, if possible.

"I would like you to check and see if the video store has any of these," Chuck said, giving me a list of movies he was looking for. "If they do, please let me know how much, and I'll send you back in to buy them."

"No problem," I said with a nod. Then, I said, "Hey, wait a sec. If you can't go into the mall because you're carnies, doesn't that apply to me, too?"

Chuck shook his head. "You? No. you have the kids—I

was told by security you are a special case. John, however...." his words trailed, and I bristled.

I marched into the mall.

John, not able to go into the mall? He had been with me at this mall since we had arrived in 2006. The mall has a great children's club, and all three kids belonged. We had many good times in the stores and the indoor playground here. A lot of special events, at least three a month, made for a great time. Not come into the mall, because he's now a carnie? Just...crazy.

I did bow to the rules in the end, however, and made runs into the mall for those who wanted this or that. A few folks challenged the rule, and most of them were actually fired after the fair's end at this site, over some possibly made-up minor infraction. I implored John, however difficult it was for him, to stay out of the mall. I would continue to make the runs inside.

Opening day dawned bright and clear, the temperatures quite pleasant still for the end of March.

It amazed me, while I made the rounds with water bottles, how each fair was different. Walking around was made easier, much easier, on pavement than on mud, but setup seemed a bit longer and harder because of uneven areas. The rides needed to be level, and it was a spectacle in itself to watch just how the carnies would handle it. Giant "legs" sprouted on each side of all the rides at different levels. But when they were tested, they ended up rock solid and straight. In one way, it was an abstract artist's dream of squiggly lines, neon lights, and monster rides.

My niece came down to visit me at the grounds one day during the week. She got a wonderful gift—any ride she wanted, as many times as she liked, for free. My sister and my eldest, Joseph, enjoyed the rides too. And I was granted a greater gift still—Amber and I started talking once more. That was comforting, and eased the heartache I had had over it quite a bit.

John took his breaks, as he always did, when he knew I was at the fair. He would call me to ask where I was, and he took the kids on the rides. It was only for about an hour, but he enjoyed that hour as best as he could, and in the way he loved the most. With his kids, having fun.

At the church on teardown Sunday, I talked about how things were going, what life was like in the carnival world. A bit shocking to the congregation, as I told them about how there were a few new people that openly tried to do drugs, and were quickly admonished by others not to do it in mine or the kids' presence. Several had come to me for prayer or Bible study, or simply just to enjoy a pleasant conversation without worrying about who was dating whom, what was going on in the next tent, or some kind of gossip that was running rampant. We had witnessed were a few fights, quickly broken up by security. No harm had come to me and the children the whole time we were with this company. Many in the congregation horrified that we had lived in a tent with the two kids. I asked, how is it different from camping at this time of the year? We were on a mission. What missionaries in the world didn't face a little danger in the countries they served? The kids had playtime and were well supervised. There were only two carnies that I trusted enough to watch the kids when I had to make a trip to the bathroom. At all other times I was constantly at the kids' sides.

But I also told them of the progress that had been made. I took carnies to the store or the laundromat when they needed to go. Sometimes it was late at night, but John would stay with the kids, or he would drive the guys himself. That was how we got to know many of the carnies' stories, and hear their testimonies. Several sat with us and talked about the Bible at the Bible study Scott and John had arranged. There was also another bonus—Chad and I were able to set up a movie night twice a week, in the open air pavilion where the meals were eaten during the winter/off season. There were only four people at first, but the idea had caught on and we had a full house. Each night someone brought out a DVD player, and we watched a good movie, usually a comedy and rated PG. Only soda was allowed, and if people wanted to smoke, they had to walk away to do it, then return.

There were no fights allowed, and often someone came out with chips, popcorn and soda to share. It was a nice time. We all got together to laugh and have fun, without the drama that was the norm.

Sadly, some people never seemed to leave their high school antics and attitude behind. Rumors flew about people, and about us. At one time a rumor circulated that I was not feeding the kids. My favorite rumor was that John ran a harem, and I wasn't allowed to sleep in the bunkhouse. I was angry inside, but gave it to God, and simply laughed when I was told. I wanted to show it didn't bother me, at least on the outside, and kept going about my business. The rumors soon died, though the grim-looking women that did the cooking and made the accusations did their best to try and conjure up more. Everyone else knew the truth, and soon, no one else would listen to them.

"If God is with me, what man, or woman in this case, can stand against me?" I asked everyone. "His word is truth, and the truth shall shine a light to dispel the darkness. I am not afraid," I added. "Their words cannot hurt me."

The congregation then made plans for the night. There was a lot to do, and a short time to do it in. The ladies' Bible study group and the youth group were going to team up to make sandwiches, not only peanut butter and jelly, but different cold meats and cheese. There would also be a variety of snack stuff, potato chips, pretzels, cookies and more. The cups of soup, coffee, tea, and water would be present, along with juice and milk in a cooler.

For most of the night, the youth group was going to be running the table under the supervision of the Pastor and his wife, with some of the elders taking shifts through the night and next morning. Everyone was coming early, around seven, so they could enjoy some of the fair, too.

We met at seven on the dot, at the edge of the midway, and walked toward the office booths. Unfortunately, not everyone in upper management was in support of the churches' hosting teardown, and a churlish man rudely told us that not only was he not going to give the youth groups admission bracelets, but what business did we have, feeding these people for free? He was in the middle of telling me off, in fact, when the main supervisor intervened, giving the man his own what for.

"These people are here to help us," he said angrily. "I don't know what your resistance is, but these people are doing something good for us all. That includes you, by the way."

"I don't need no charity," the man replied. "And these are only carnies. Half of them are criminals, the other half, society rejects, and—"

"And they're still people," replied the main supervisor.

"I know you are friends with my father, who ran this rat race. And yeah, some of them are halfwits out here. BUT—" he pointed to us, "These are good people, who only wish to help. Nothing wrong with that, and it's starting to do some good."

The man quickly apologized, and we went to the office window to speak to another man about the bracelets. The gentleman there, a kind, older fellow, heard the commotion, and told us to meet him around the back of the cart. We did, and everyone finally got their bracelets for the ride.

At closing time, tables and chairs were brought out. One of the elder's vans was parked nearby, so I could lay the kids in it when they would fall asleep. The table was quickly set, and coffee made, as the temperature dropped and the wind picked up.

Everyone gathered in a circle, and the Pastor led us in prayer.

"Dear Heavenly Father," he began. "We thank you for this opportunity to reach out to others, and to spread your word. There are many souls here that have heard the good news, and are starting to respond to your blessings. We thank you, Heavenly Father, for the protection you have provided for Jackie and John and their children, while they are in the mission field. We ask for your protection also for these men and women, as they take down these rides tonight."

It was nice to sit in a chair this time, as every other teardown was spent on my feet or sitting on the ground. It was also great to have the company of those I know so well around me. I thanked them all for participating, and told the youth group this would be an education they would not soon forget, once the rides started coming down.

True to those words, everyone, even the adults present, had their mouths open at the sight of the precarious positions everyone took in order to bring down the giant machines. We were just across from the Ring of Fire, and for the first time, I got to watch John with his work. Everyone stared and held his breath, silently saying prayers as John stood on the three-foot-wide flat spot on top of that circle, to begin bringing it down.

"Every teardown they do this?" asked the Pastor, his eyes never leaving John's form.

"Yes," I replied. "The last spot, it rained, and he was on top."

"He is confident," observed another.

I smiled. "That is because he walks, and works, with God on his side."

The youth group was simply mesmerized, and gasped as the circle started folding in on itself. John was now standing perfectly still, having half of that flat spot he stood on taken away. In the blink of an eye he scaled down the ladder to undo the second latch.

On the opposite side, we could view several different rides. I wanted to take the kids in the youth group on a brief tour to see the different rides, and devised a way to do it. We were going to distribute water, and we took three kids at a time with us on each run. Everyone would come away with a different perspective and respect for the carnies by the end of the night. The kids asked questions bout the rides, which were answered by the crew chiefs. It was encouraging to see the kids so interested in something, and see the other side of the fun they had.

The wind made the work a little rougher, but we were somewhat sheltered by the elder's van flanking one end of the tables, and the office trailer we were backed up against, which was the only place we could hook up for coffee and hot water.

"It didn't take very long for us to make these sandwiches," Ms. Connie said. "There were five of us ladies. Two of us worked on the PBJ's, two worked on the meat and cheese. The last stuffed them in the baggies and marked what kind of sandwich it was."

"Yes, and we men went shopping," laughed Pastor Ron. "It didn't take us long to select the chips and snack stuff, or the bottled water and coffee. We really didn't buy much, because we had a lot of it stocked in the food pantry already."

I nodded. "Just goes to show, I guess, that to do something for another is actually easy. You don't need a lot of money, or a lot of people, really."

"And it takes someone who cares enough to get it going, with God's direction, to the right people that will help make it grow," finished the Pastor.

I nodded. "Exactly. If only the rest of the world would catch on to that." I glanced around, doing a quick headcount. "If ten people can do it, imagine what the world would be like, if everyone did something?"

"That would mirror Heaven," said one of the elders.

"It doesn't even need to be a few people," said another. "Look at what you have done by yourself."

I blushed and shook my head. "Nah. It's a team effort. Always has been."

Everyone grinned, and just shook their heads, getting ready for the line of men that were heading for the table.

Hunter and Rozeanna were fast asleep, when around two o'clock hit—which seemed to be the witching hour for me. I snoozed upright in a chair once more, and someone covered me with a blanket. Some of the youth group were in the van with the kids, and they were checked on every so often.

Through the night, as people came up for the treats, they personally thanked and shook the hands of everyone at the table. They were aware that this was the church we had come from, and were grateful for the church in Kissimmee who did the Osceola Fair, and who had helped as they could with food runs and other things throughout. A few took a break to discuss the Bible in reference to what we were doing, and two people asked to be witnessed and saved that night. One was a man who hadn't been to church and was skeptical of God for many years. It was an exhilarating experience to witness the inner change in some folks.

It wasn't until the light mist began falling around dawn that I awoke.

"Good morning," said the Pastor. "Connie went home to get some sleep, as did most of the youth group. Frankie was here for a bit, and he was just thrilled at everything going on."

I smiled. Frankie was some character, and I loved his enthusiasm. He and his wife, Stevie, were quite the pair, and excited about the Lord. The two were involved in anything that would praise the Lord, and I could just imagine him giving his testimony—wide eyed, absorbing everything, and praising and asking God every second for their safety, for the good they were doing, for the word being heard. It was something that I was sorry I missed!

I helped the Pastor make coffee, and, with the arrival of another member of the congregation, filled a cart and went out to distribute water once more. It amazed me that the rides came down so quickly this time around, and only a few of the heavy duty thrill rides were still under deconstruction. John, I had found out, finished his ride at three, helped tear down another, then went to sleep in the car.

Noon time, and all but one ride was finished. The Pastor told me the supplies were depleted too, and came to help me distribute the last of the food and drink we had. He too, was amazed how quickly the men worked, and said he felt good that the church's presence may have helped them have a good night. I totally agreed.

Back at Winter Quarters, the next three weeks were spent running people to the laundromat, the grocery stores, and the bus stop. Some were leaving for other venues, a few inspired to go home and better their lives, thanks to our ministry. John was away for the next month, working "Mall Spots," with a only few rides, and no place for me and the kids to stay. Phone calls were made, too, and at least two churches hosted a tear down while they were on the Mall runs. Everyone did treat us with respect at this show, and made sure anyone who was new did the same. Chad and Blaze were in charge of looking out for me and the kids. I met several times with Wendy, who was instrumental in gathering food. The rest of the crew were working on the rides, maintaining them for the second half of the season, which would run from New York State back to Florida.

At the end of the three weeks, I moved back into my parents' house with the kids, since John had decided to switch shows. Christ for Carnies, was about to expand. Chad and many others were sad to see us go, but we promised to keep in touch with them and other friends we made, and we still talk to them this day.

– 7 –
Starting Over

I drove John up to Virginia and stayed for three days to get him settled in his new home. This was a painful time for us—now he would truly be away for the rest of the year. I didn't like it; neither of us did. But jobs in his field were still scarce, and he had an offer at least, with a little more pay. John was happy, though; he was originally from New Jersey, and this company had a stop just a few moments down the road from where he lived.

As soon as we arrived, I explained to a few people about Christ for Carnies and what we did. Just because I couldn't be present for many of their runs didn't mean it had to shut down. I was still working with the Florida show, making calls to churches in every area they were going to play. Scott ending up joining John at the bigger show, and at least I knew my husband wouldn't be alone.

But for now I concentrated on my husband and my children. We had a coupon for Build-a-Bear Workshop®, a thank-you for having Rozeanna's birthday party there the year before. We took the kids, and I videotaped John and Rozeanna making a wish and put those wishes in the teddy bear's heart. Rozeanna took an extra one, and made me cry by making a wish and giving it to daddy to carry with him when they were gone. They named their creation Carnie Bear.

It was not easy to leave. Rozeanna cried all the way through Virginia and part of the way into South Carolina, until she fell asleep. Hunter cried because Rozeanna was crying. I cried silently, just watching the road.

Arriving back at my parent's house, the life of the single married mom began once again. I juggled the responsibility of caring for the kids with writing down my memories, going out twice a week to the Florida show to help until they left, helping with the church activities, and just enjoying my kids and time with my relatives.

I am forever grateful that in God's infinite wisdom, he paved the way for me to come home and enjoy those last few weeks, for in the beginning of June came the day all of us had dreaded for the past twenty-plus years.

Mom and Dad drove back up home to Springfield, Massachusetts for their yearly summer visit, two weeks after I got back from dropping off John. Mom was getting a little slower, I had noticed, and this concerned me. Her sudden burst of energy to drive the twenty-four-hour trip was a good thing to see, but I couldn't shake a feeling of foreboding when they left the house. I was alone now; everyone was out of state with the coming of June, and for the first time I wasn't sure what to do. Phone calls to different state churches had been made, and except for the occasional confirmation, pep talk or information a hosting church would need, I was idle.

After two weeks came the dreaded news.

"Your mother is in the hospital," Dad said quietly. I was upset, but she had been there before, many, many times. "How is she doing?"

Silence.

"Dad? How is she doing?" I asked again.

"Not good," was the reply. "Be ready. You kids might have to come up here, soon."

I asked what had happened. Mom was having a good time, laughing and talking to everyone that came to visit—her brother, nieces, nephews, a few high school friends—one moment, and couldn't catch her breath the next. At the hospital, the doctors told her she had to have a trachea tube. If she didn't, she would be dead within the hour.

I nodded and hung up the phone, shaking. I started finding flights to Massachusetts...just in case. Mom had been at death's door before, once when she was nine months pregnant with my youngest brother, and had always pulled through. I sent up a silent prayer that this was the case.

The next day Dad called again. The news wasn't good. Happily, my relationship with Amber had mended, and again I credit God's wisdom and knowledge of what is best for us. Rozeanna went that night to stay at my friend's house. My cousin, Hunter and I took a flight to Boston.

Mom looked worse than I had ever seen her. Still, I had hope until the end. This woman was such a huge influence in my life. Yes, we butted heads often, and even got into occasional screaming matches. But she was my mother, and she sacrificed over the years. The courage she had to face every day, knowing she had a limited time, and live life to the fullest while praising God is a book in itself.

A pastor in Springfield came and prayed for my mother. I told my her that I very much wanted her to live, to see her grandchildren grow healthy and strong. But if it was God's will that she should go home now, to go in peace to his loving arms. Grandpa, Aunt Sue, Aunt Mary and a few others were waiting for her, and she could watch over her grandkids as an angel in Heaven. I told her I loved her very much, and then left the room.

Mom went home to Heaven at 4:10 a.m., June 20th, 2009.

John was not able to be by my side during this time. The carnival had arrived in New Jersey, but there was no time off for a recent hire like John. I had to face this one alone, in many ways.

I took a few days to reflect on things, how happy I was that mom had come to her hometown and got to say goodbye to all that she loved. As I walked the grounds of my grandmother's house, I saw the ghosts of the six generations of family that had lived or visited there. So many good times, a few tragic. Yet, it felt as though another page in the book of life had turned, and I thought about the unknown future that faced me and the children on the plane ride home.

Depression set in, and the Christ for Carnies ministry suffered for a week. I felt lost, without direction, for the first time in a long time. My daily routine just seemed mechanical. I went to visit my son Joseph, who lived with his father, desperately needing to feel connected to my kids.

After two weeks I left for New Jersey. I was going to my closest friend and my husband, who was working at the

New Jersey State Fair.

I arrived on July 7th. I didn't tell John I was coming to celebrate our second anniversary. Scott knew, and orchestrated the surprise. I stopped to pick up my friend Arlene, who lived only a half hour away from where the state fair was held. We arrived just after the close of the fair. It was a rough trip to say the least, with two little ones, especially with Rozeanna starting to potty train. Nighttime was the best time to travel, when they slept.

But I was there, parked a few spots away where I could see the door to the bunkhouse. I called Scott. John took the phone and wished me a happy anniversary.

"I wish we were together to celebrate it," he said softly.

That just made me grin, as he walked into view of my hiding spot. "Wish on a star, John...you never know what will happen."

Arlene was trying hard not to giggle, telling the kids to *shhhh....*

"I'm closing my eyes," John said. "And I'm wishing to God that we were together right now."

I slipped out of the car. "Look behind you."

John opened his eyes and gave me that smile I so love, and the one that gets him out of a lot of doghouses. He ran up to me and spun me around.

"Oh, my God!" he cried. "When did you get here? Where are the kids?"

I just laughed and kissed him deeply, pointing to the car just a few spots over, where Arlene was getting out and laughing. Many of the folks around us, Scott included, were clapping.

"We knew all along, man," Scott said with a grin.

"You guys hungry?" I asked. "We're going out to eat."

"Do we have the money?" John asked. I nodded. So we squeezed John and Scott into the car, and made a short trip down to the nearest diner to celebrate. Part of the conversation included condolences from Scott and John, and I caught them up on several carnie folks. Some had been released from the show in Florida and ended up homeless for a week or so on the street in Orlando. I had come by as often as I could to see that they were fed and not forgotten. After Mom had died, I heard they found their way north to another show. We all prayed that they were OK.

"What now?" Scott asked.

I shrugged. "Well, I'm going to stay at Arlene's house for a little while, try to get a job."

"What about the mission?" he asked.

I shrugged. "I don't know."

I truly didn't know what would happen. I wanted to continue, but there was nothing to do in Florida right now. I had to leave. It seemed as though a chapter had closed, and I felt lost, depressed, sad. I wasn't sure what to do next.

"Hey, look, we're so close to New York City," John said, turning to me. "Why don't we go into the city for a while? And maybe we can squeeze in the Statue of Liberty," he added, taking my hand. "You always wanted to see it, and it *is* our anniversary."

Arlene and Scott nodded, and plans were made. The guys came back with us to Arlene's parent's house. She lived with them and they were our dear friends. Family, actually, of the heart. I spent the night with my husband, for the first time in months, in the basement bedroom of my friend's home.

New York City vibrated and hummed with its usual energy when we stepped out of Penn Station. It was only the second time I had ever been to the city. John and Arlene grew up just minutes away and had been there several times, including on 9/11. But the city had never lost its beat, giving those who came to see her the ultimate adrenaline rush. It felt good to do something different, something for us. Rozeanna and Hunter, who looked at the city with wide, curious eyes, were happy to have their "cousins," Arlene's daughters, Daisy and Dixie, by their side.

Times Square, Rockefeller Center, Fifth Avenue and Central Park all have a way of lifting the spirits, and got me smiling despite my sadness. We paused to take a few wonderful shots at every place we could think of, and had lunch in Times Square with the guys. Their day ended a little too early, though, as they had to take the train back to the Meadowlands, and get ready to work once more.

Arlene, the kids and I decided to stay for a little while longer, exploring Central Park. Arlene, my oldest friend and one of two sisters of my heart. If it weren't for her, I wouldn't have met John, have had two more great kids, and be so in love. I thank her for that, forever.

We talked as we walked through the park, hearing the kids laughing.

"What do you plan to do?" Arlene asked. "I mean, you're welcome to stay as long as you like. You know that."

I nodded.

"I know you're upset," Arlene continued. "and I am sorry your mom died. I...." her words trailed off.

I gave her a hug, and thanked her for caring. The answer would come soon, but just then, I needed time for me.

The sun set as we crossed back over the city, the girls tired out from a wonderful day at the park. They were hungry, however, and we stopped at New York Deli for a light snack to hold us over until we got back to the house. We did not go to the fair that night, and the guys slept in their bunks.

I lay awake looking at the ceiling, talking to God. I was so grateful for this little bit of family time. John would soon be gone again, traveling to New York, Ohio, then Tennessee and other points south. I couldn't stay forever. I didn't want to stay with anyone—I wanted to be on our own once more. I shook my head, and turned over to get to sleep.

Lady Liberty makes a big impression on everyone, and it is very exciting to see the statue for the very first time. Each one of us took a pause to reflect, however, when we saw a simple memorial to the Twin Towers. We were lost in our own thoughts about that horrid day.

I was in Boston, experiencing the after-effects of a city-wide evacuation after copycat bomb scares were reported and military air planes filled the air. I was supposed to be there with Joseph, sightseeing near the towers on that day, while a friend had an interview on the 30th floor of Tower 2. My friend was there, but he survived.

Scott was in Buffalo, and like Arlene, who was home, watched the events unfold on their sets.

John was on a roof nearby somewhere in Manhattan, then on a boathouse right in the bay, getting a live view of a day in hell. John's sister was in the lobby of the first tower hit, and was rescued by a brave security guard who smashed the glass to get everyone out.

I was thankful to God that those standing with me were not harmed on that fateful day.

We then turned and bought our tickets, making ready to board the ferry and at long last see the Statue of Liberty up close. There was a brief stop at Ellis Island, and the photographer in me couldn't resist jumping off and snapping a few shots while they unloaded and reloaded passengers.

When the ferry came around the bend, there was the Lady in all her glory, the sun's rays filtering through the clouds to light up the torch. I suddenly felt like an immigrant, coming from a foreign country, with just the clothes on my back, with my children and my husband, and a pocket full of dreams. The first few lines of Lee Greenwood's famous song, "God Bless the USA," one of my favorites, came to mind.

It was true—we were starting over, in many, many ways. A new life before us, and adventure awaited. I was inspired, and took more pictures of that statue and all that surrounds her.

It was when we were getting ready to rejoin the ferry in the afternoon that Arlene noticed the tall flag pole behind Lady Liberty. She went over to get a shot. I turned to ask her a question to find her gone, and my eyes followed her form, curious. When she came back, Arlene issued me a challenge.

"I got a picture of the flag and the statue together, back to back," she said. "But it was hard." She grinned. "Can you get one?"

I was off, yelling, "Heck yeah, I can," and went to the back where she was standing, turned and looked through the view finder. The challenges presented themselves immediately, and I dropped to my knees.

Still not enough.

People must have thought I was a bit nutty, as I got lower to the ground, trying several positions, which included lying on my stomach, then resting my head on the curb while lying on my back, to get that shot.

I was starting to lift out of my depression, just a little.

Arlene, the girls, my kids and I went to visit the state fair that night. We got an admission pass, with free rides, which was really great.

This show was three times as big as the one in Florida, and had different units in different places. We went to visit Scott on the wave swinger, then to the Ferris wheel, and then the kiddy rides, where John was in charge of a kid roller coaster called the Go Gator.

It impressed me how well he did his job, as we stood observing him at work. He showed concern for the children as he made sure they were the proper height. He showed sadness when he shook his head to let parents know their child was too short to ride. Tears welled in his eyes each time a child cried, and he told the parents he was sorry, but even his own daughter was too small to go on the ride.

Rozeanna broke free from my grasp and ran toward him, wrapping her little arms around John's neck. I and smiled at the annoyed parents, who couldn't understand why an inch or so of height was such a big deal. John and I seemed to change a few people's minds that night, and it was good to help people come away with a different understanding.

If children are not tall enough, they run the risk of the seat belt's not fitting right, an injury risk. Too short, and they could literally bounce out of the seat, no matter how tight the belt, because it would not be secure around the waist. Too tall, and the harsh bouncing of the hills of the coaster will injure the spine of a child.

A ride might also be restricted because of too much weight on one side, as in the case of the Ferris wheel. If there's not enough weight distributed evenly, the wheel will not climb and complete its circle. Or, on other rides like the Fireball, you won't fit in the seat properly if you are too large in the front— the harness that locks you in the seat will make it difficult to breathe. Something that is hard to hear, yes. No one wants to hear that he or she is too big, too tall, or too busty for anything. But, believe me, these folks tell us for our own safety that, and endure the tongue lashing and vindictive complaints to management they often receive with a polite smile.

John's dad met us at the fair that night, visiting his grandchildren for the first time in three-and-a-half years. He was overjoyed that he had a grandson to carry on the family name. Grandpa stuck with us for a while, going on the rides with Rozeanna, Daisy and Dixie.

Many people by now had found out about what we had done in Florida, through both John and Scott.

"That *is* something," the carnies said, as soon as they found out I was John's wife. "I don't think I ever really heard of one person doing so much."

As before, I blushed, and reminded them it was a team effort—God, myself, and the churches that were involved.

"With us, once your ride is down, you go to sleep," someone else told me. "Unless you volunteer to help tear down more, or you're a supervisor of a section. I nodded, listening. Every show had a different way of doing things, it seemed.

Teardown night came, but it still wasn't in my heart to do anything...not to mention I didn't have much time. Arlene and I went out with the kids to say goodbye to the guys the next day, and then John was gone again.

Daisy, Dixie, Hunter and Roze in Central Park

Hunter, Rozeanna, and John with me at Build-A-Bear Workshop

- 8 -
RETURN TO THE MISSION

A month flew by like the wind when it blows the leaves in autumn. It was nice to stay at Arlene's, letting Rozeanna enjoy being with Daisy and Dixie, and letting her experience things like running through sprinklers. We also got to know John's family very well, and I was especially glad to connect with John's mom, Marie. She was not only a lifesaver for taking over our car payment and giving John and me a phone from her family cell account; she became a true friend. I am forever grateful, not only for Arlene's mom, but also for my mother-in-law being there for us in so many ways.

I continued doing what I could for the mission over the phone and with the Internet. I took time for kids and myself to heal, and wonder where we were going to start over again. I was hoping it would be New Jersey, with its endless opportunities for entertainment for both children and adults, along with its proximity to New York City. And there were people I loved in New Jersey. I had known Arlene's parents, Aimee and Rick, for around seven years. They were so close to my heart I called them Mama Bear and Papa Bear, because they're Chicago Bear fans. I needed that now more than ever, that connection to family.

John and Scott were in Ohio, in the middle of one of the biggest plays for the show, the Ohio State Fair. We talked almost every night when he got off work. The conversation lasted maybe ten minutes: "Hi, honey, how are you? The kids did what?....Ok, gotta go, I'm tired. Love you." But they were precious, and something I looked forward to every day.

Mama Bear did her best to encourage me, and tried to help me find a job, child care, and other things we would need to settle in New Jersey. I was having no luck. In such a crazy economy, employers had the power, and they were extra choosy when hiring a new employee. Not that I didn't have the potential or the credentials, but I didn't have a full bachelors' degree or ten years experience. It's a sad world where no one wishes to take the time to train anyone, or values employees with families, but worships the almighty dollar.

But my issues weren't about all that. My issue was that I missed my husband, and time for my stay was growing short. I could continue to bunk at Arlene's, but the house was crowded as it was. Hunter slept in a playpen, I slept on a loveseat, and Rozeanna on a air mattress on the floor.

School was coming too, and Rozeanna was school age. What would I do then? Too many questions, and not enough answers. Everything, it seemed, was on hold, until the day I watched a movie based on the true story of my ultimate inspiration for writing, Laura Ingalls Wilder, and her daughter, Rose.

I watched the movie, fascinated by the heartache and dangers that the famous pioneer woman endured. I was a huge fan of the show, even to the point of introducing the reruns to all three of my children. One day, I vowed to make it to the Missouri farm she and "Manly" spent most of their days. I also admired the love between Laura and Manly, and how they kept each other strong. The same was true with John and me. In the face of adversity, we both stood strong. And I knew we had to stand together, and finish what we had started. My thoughts were interrupted by an argument erupting between the kids.

They were arguing more and more every day, and Rozeanna was becoming unhappy that she couldn't go to school when the time came. I sighed, calmed them all down, and went to ask Mama Bear what to do.

We decided to go for a cup of coffee at The Reo, a famous restaurant in Woodbridge, and somewhere we visited often.

The Reo was once called the Highway Diner, back in the mid-nineteen-thirties. The name was changed in 1940 thanks to the car, the Reo Runabout, and has stuck ever since. Voted the best in Central Jersey for years, the gem of Woodbridge, famous throughout the world, was always a place where good friends met to eat.

Mama Bear greeted the night manager warmly as she had for many years. The diner was always pleasant and always packed, no matter the time of day or night, and as the pictures on the wall behind the checkout counter proved, it was a popular place with many celebrities of the local and world-famous kind. This night was no exception.

"I think the time has come for me to leave," I said quietly, sipping my coffee. "Roze will be a wreck when the girls are gone all day long."

"Where would you go?" she asked.

"The only place I can go," I told her. "With John."

"How will you live?" she asked, now giving me her full attention. "You have food stamps, but didn't you just spend the last of them last night?"

"We'll get by, somehow," I told her. "Daisy needs her own room back, and...my kids need their father."

"And you need your husband," Arlene finished.

I only nodded. "Yes."

"When are you going to leave?" she asked.

"Tomorrow."

Mama Bear gave me a hug, the kind of hug a mother gives a daughter, and just what I needed at that moment.

"Be safe," she whispered.

At four o'clock the next afternoon, I pulled out of the drive, and hit the road once more, heading for Tennessee.

There was a pit stop I had to make first. Four hours from where my second family lived was a small town in the West Virginia panhandle called, "Gerrardstown." I stopped there to connect to a piece of my history. In the 1700s, my eighth great-grandfather, Reverend Gerrard, became the first pastor to come over the Blue Ridge Mountains. His son laid out the tracts of land to develop the town. Many other relatives went on to Pennsylvania to Gerrard's Fort, and Gerrard's Station in Ohio. There was another town called Gerrard, but the name had to be changed to Inwood to avoid confusion when the post office was established. I stood with the kids, speaking a silent tribute to the house and church they lived and prayed in that still stands today.

I knew little about my biological father, and it was during that summer I started learning who I really was. Now, as I turned the car south, I left my past behind me. I headed toward my future, and though I didn't know what it would bring, I knew God would stand with me.

The road journey was a long and frightful one for me. All day long I drove through Virginia, then another four hours into Tennessee, finally arriving on a Thursday morning. I told John I was coming this time around, and he said he had a bed ready for us. I had no idea what to expect, but I already had a vision. In my mind's eye, Christ for Carnies was back on track, and I was going to arrive with my newfound faith in things and spread kindness and God's word.

We were not so far from Nashville in this spot, and I made sure to take a day and drive around. We didn't have much money left. Now it was truly paycheck to paycheck, calling for frugalness and ingenuity. We did have a problem—we had two weeks to go before the food stamps would arrive again. I left New Jersey with some food and water, and relied once again on the lesson of loaves and fishes to make it last.

Sadly, Scott had had to leave because of an emergency at home. For the first time, we were truly on our own, starting over.

Rozeanna flew into the arms of her father, I into the arms of my husband. Hunter, however, took a look at his father, now again a stranger, and cried his little heart out. *My heart sank.* Well, time would change that. We only spent a few hours together before John had to go to work, but I was happy. We were together again.

One of the great things about traveling was that we got to see places we never thought we would, and learn about places far beyond the bubble we grew up and grew old in. Here, the blinders were taken off, and we found out how small and how big the world was at the same time.

I started out with the mission once more, right away. I had some bottles of water, and decided to give some out to the people around John's section. I was saving back a case for us. I thanked God too, that I breastfed Hunter—I could not imagine the nightmare if we had to buy formula. I was also determined to find old towels at thrift stores when the diapers ran out and make cloth diapers for him, too.

People looked at me a little funny when I offered them some water, and I actually had a few bottles left. I left the area that John was working, and went on to explore the fair.

It would take a few days for people to realize who I was, but it seemed my reputation had preceded me. They began to accept my offers to do their laundry, to give them a ride down to the store, to pray with them if they should need it. I tried to find a church to host a teardown for the coming Sunday, but I met with resistance this time around, and wondered what to do.

After one heavy storm in Wilsonburg, I was out as usual to let Rozeanna ride on the rides. The sky was grey and a light mist still clung to the air, but provided me with an incredible opportunity for a photograph. A beautiful rainbow appeared in the sky, and as I pointed the camera upward, one of the bigger thrill rides arced upward into my viewfinder. I blinked. The rainbow seemed to beam out of each end of the ride. I framed up and waited a few seconds more for the ride to complete its circular course, and fired away at the shutter. The carnival ride and the rainbow, God's promise, seemed to symbolize our mission.

Teardown came, and I sat reading the Bible while the kids slept, and prepared for the next jump, the city of Memphis.

The Memphis sun beat brutally down on everyone as we waited in the grass under a bit of shade for the bunkhouse to arrive. Everyone by now had gotten to know and love the kids, and the carnies came over to talk to us. We were not fools, though, and we kept the kids with us at all times. We made a few new friends, and cemented some friendships that had already started. Sadly, we made some enemies as well, though we didn't know it just yet. The supervisor was skeptical to say the least, but I made sure we did nothing to give him cause to boot us from the show.

We were given a bunk house that night by one of the supervisors. This did not sit well with the bunkhouse coordinator, a young, angry young man who sneered as we unpacked the car and did what we could to make the bunk presentable at that time of night.

"Whoa, look at that!" he hollered to a crowd that had gathered. "Here comes the trailer trash, boys!"

I frowned. The words stung and I let them hurt me. I am human, after all. I argued, which didn't look well for a representative of a fledgling ministry. But it did win me respect, as far as the carnie world was concerned.

This bunkhouse was a little bigger than the last show's, but still a small box. If you have never seen them, imagine this. Take a tractor trailer, and make five rooms out of it, with two bunk beds, shelves at the end of a bunk, and anchored to the wall near the head of the bed. Storage is underneath the bottom bunk. The dimensions? Ten feet high, eight feet long, and approximately four feet wide. At least this box had air conditioning, a small window in the door, and a bonus—a solid, locking metal door. At the end of the trailer was a common shower for that particular bunk house. Rough metal stairs jutted out from the door to the ground, and the walls were thin.

This was a far cry from my dream of the little white house with a picket fence.

It became very difficult to juggle the two kids as Hunter got older and more mobile. But we continued on for the mission. In the morning, it was nice and cool with a lot of shade between the row of bunkhouses. Hunter was in the shade in his playpen, and Rozeanna would play quietly right in front of him, or sit with pen and paper. I would read the Bible to them, and to anyone who wished. By the third, a small group of four people would bring their chairs and surround our steps to listen to the Word.

Enemies, however, did everything they could to disturb the good word. More than once, someone brought out a drug and offered it to those who were in the circle. I did not stop, instead, I continued to read. I started choosing chapters that talked about salvation for the wicked, and the only pause or recognition I gave, was to ask the question, "Hello. Did you come to get saved today?" Those words, chased them right back out.

Our days were filled going shopping, doing laundry, letting the kids play, reading books and or the Bible, then going out to the fair and letting Roze ride the rides once more.

Danger came in different forms. One small train ride Roze was on derailed going around the corner in a shower of sparks. I screamed and was up over the gate, but I was overtaken by a supervisor who had seen the situation. Roze and the other children were OK, but my heart was indeed in my throat and I praised God for watching out for her. Every time I drove I prayed the entire way, including on a trip to downtown Memphis. I thought people in Orlando moved fast, but these folks racing down the highway made the I-4 Highway in central Florida look like a Sunday drive.

John also had his problems. He was passed over for a supervisor's position in favor of someone he had trained and who had only joined at the last stop. A carnie threatened to beat the "do-gooder" to a pulp in front of his kids. John and I asked each other what we could do to get out of this, but no option presented itself. We could only cling to our faith in God that an answer would come.

Fortunately, we had as many friends as we had enemies. A few days away from the food stamps coming in, we were down to our last bottle of water. John told me he would get water somewhere to give to the kids. I remembered the Pastor talking about an orphanage director who relied solely on donations. There were times the children and he sat at an empty table, and would thank the Lord anyway for their daily bread. No sooner would the prayer finish, when a knock at the door would reveal a kind stranger who was moved by the hand of God to cook for them.

I nodded, and thought that lesson was a wonderful one. We were going through rough days, but if it weren't for God, we wouldn't have any days at all.

"Dear Heavenly Father, we thank you for every day that you have given us, for the time we spend together. It may not be in a luxury hotel, or even the comfort of a living room, but it is here, in this little box, that we are together, and that is the most important part of all. Thank you Lord, for I may miss the things we don't have, but what is more important are the things we do have. Our health. A roof over our heads. Food. " I glanced down. "And this one bottle of water. Amen."

What happened next is the truth. I got ready to open the water and divide it into the kids' sippy cups, when we heard a knock on the door. It was one of our friends, an older man in his fifties, carrying a case of water on his back.

"I went to the store for a few supplies for myself," he said as I opened the door, "and had a feeling you might be needing this. Even if you don't, you will soon," He added.

I took the water from him, sat it down on the floor, and gave him a hug from the heart as I cried.

"Thank you for being an angel," I told him. "I just finished praying to the Lord, thanking him for our last bottle, when you came."

One has to marvel that this man, who was in poor health, did such a good deed. The nearest store to carry water was a good five miles down the road, and the temperature soared to the high nineties, low hundreds, before you even considered the humidity. This man had no car, no bike, not even a cart to pull the water. He carried it on his shoulder, much like Jesus carried the cross.

One night, right after everyone came in from work, I sat on the steps eating a late dinner with John. A commotion rang out near the portable toilets when one of the workers who came to clean them fell to the ground. Two men performed CPR for the forty-five minutes it took for an ambulance to arrive. John and I quickly formed a prayer chain to pray for a recovery for the man, or the acceptance of his soul to Heaven, and for strength for the loved ones he would leave behind. Sadly, it was the latter, and I looked at John with concern. I worried a little less, but I still would not want him to die here, like this.

Teardown came quickly, and I knew what I was going to do. Taking our only coffee pot, crock pot and electric skillet, I borrowed a table from one of the games, and set up a simple spaghetti dinner for whoever wished to have some.

Now, the bunkhouse coordinator who'd called us trailer trash and caused more than a few arguments had grown quiet in the last week of the fair. John and I wondered at the change. The girlfriend of the guy came to her bunk, right next to ours, and was surprised to find me up at three a.m., sitting on my steps.

"Smells good," she said, sitting on her steps. "How much?"

I shrugged. "Well, I wasn't really charging," I told her, starting to fix a plate. "But people have been giving me a few dollars here and there." I smiled, handing her the plate. "Some people haven't given anything. All I really ask for is a thank you."

She grew quiet, staring at the plate, and I thought there was a glint of a tear in her eye as I handed her some cold juice. Our food stamps had arrived by now, happily, and I made sure food and drink was available. I thought of it as our tithe.

"Why would you do this?" she asked. "Why would you care? Especially about me?"

"Because I love people, I always have, " I replied. "And God loves everyone, too. I only want to show that." She rolled her eyes a little. "I am not pressing religion on anyone by saying that. I just want people to know it. I am here to spread that message. People will do with it what they will after that."

She looked at me curiously for a few moments. We sat

and talked for a good hour, she having a second plate of spaghetti to boot. I told her our story, about Christ for Carnies, about the kids. She told me about how she and her boyfriend found themselves at this show, and I gained an insight to his anger.

"You know, I'm glad we talked," she said, stuffing a few dollars in my hand. "I misjudged you. We both did. You really are a nice person," she said, smiling. I offered my hand, and she took it. "You are a *special* person. Anyone messes with you, let us know, OK?"

"OK," I replied. "If you ever need anything, please let us know too." She nodded, walked away a few paces, then turned.

"Who ever thought a plate of spaghetti would change everything?" she asked, and walked off into the night.

"Who indeed," I murmured, glancing up to the brightly lit heavens. Oh yes, God did work in mysterious ways.

John was ecstatic. He had become so speedy at his job, and he had a few guys under his supervision. They had torn down three rides in a matter of hours, and stopped for a quick dinner on their way to the other side of the fair to help tear down some more.

"I am *pumped*, Jackie," he said through mouthfuls of food. "We're doing so good. I'm going to show these people I can do it, and get that pay raise. Then we'll get a camper, and have a proper home," he said with pride. He truly believed it, and I was right with him. I worried about the kids a little, and being isolated. There had been a few kids were on the show when we arrived, but they were sadly taken away from the mother and shipped off to relatives. The young girl, who was pregnant, had a bad attitude, made worse by the loss of her kids. She eyed mine like a hawk, and I prayed for her, as well as my kids' safety. I didn't want to stay in this life forever, but I knew that God needed us here now, and I gave myself over to His will completely when I left New Jersey for Tennessee.

We left the next night, taking the long ride through two states; Georgia bound, praying the whole time.

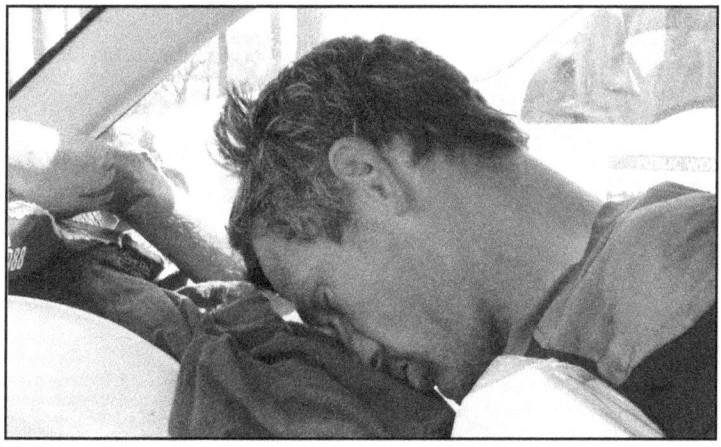

An exhausted John

Roze and Autumn, Amber's daughter   *Hunter & Roze*

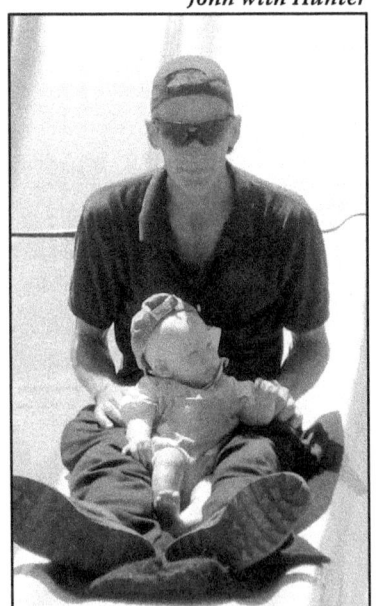
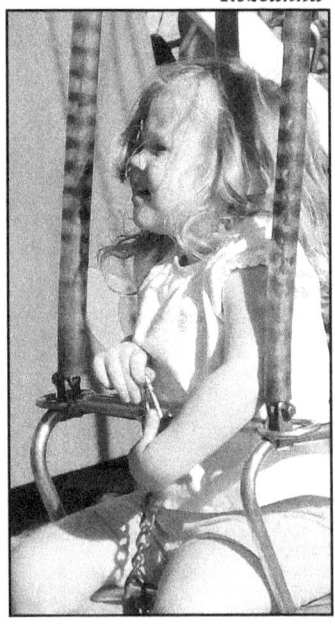

John with Hunter   *Rozeanna*

– 9 –

GEORGIA

The state known for its peaches was even hotter than Tennessee, made miserable by the constant rain that greeted us from the moment we arrived. Half of the rides and bunkhouses had not arrived yet, but one of our friends had an old van, allowing us and the kids to stretch out rather than sleep the night away in our car. Our friend's sleep was interrupted a few hours later, however, when in rode the main supervisor on a scooter, through two feet of water, banging on the side of the van and demanding that the guys come to help set up the main office tent.

I was incensed, to say the least, at the interruption of everyone's sleep, and the conditions that people were forced to work in. Police would often walk right by and did nothing. Things like that happened everywhere you looked.

We had acquired some new friends in the last days of Memphis, one a man I'll call Mark. He was tall, and a bit challenged, which made him an easy target for those we need to pray for. His heart was in the right place, though, and he walked the trek to the nearest store, a mile away every day, always asking what we wanted, and bringing us things back, whether we needed it or not.

The other friends we acquired were a husband-and-wife team. The man worked maintenance on the grounds, and the woman, one of the kiddy rides. Both were wonderful people, and very supportive. When John and the man who became his boss got engaged in a yelling match, the woman sprinted across the lot to stand with me to help stop a potential fight, even though she had been sick for over a week.

We were very close to a special doll factory, Babyland General, where the Cabbage Patch Dolls are made. I took a day off from the ministry to bring Rozeanna and Hunter there. Mom had said she would have loved to get Rozeanna one of the dolls, and I thought it fitting that the place was having a special children's celebration on Mom's birthday. I made sure to take plenty of pictures for John, who couldn't get the day off.

When I told Rozeanna that her "Honey" (what she called my Mom) was with her, and wanted her to have a special baby doll, the expression on her face brought tears to my. Rozeanna looked at all the choices available, and picked out a sweet redhead with green eyes and one tiny little tooth. I explained the situation to the staff, who were just wonderful, and let Rozeanna go through the "adoption" process. Her tiny face was serious when she took the oath to love her baby. An added bonus came when the ladies at the counter gave Roze a doll carriage. She was also amazed at the birth of a new Cabbage Patch doll from the patch itself. Rozeanna named the baby her "Honey Angel," and it was one of the happiest days of her life. I glanced up to the fading sun and thanked Mom, who I am sure had a hand in arranging such a treat with the Almighty!

The first Sunday came, and I sat out with the kids reading the Bible while John made French toast on the griddle. It was a sweet little family moment that we had on those steps, on a rare day of sunshine. Rain had hampered the opening of the fair, and had closed the fair early on both Friday and Saturday nights, their biggest money maker. I was planning on making another spaghetti plate for everyone, just to give them a little bonus, but the rain came again that night and ruined that plan.

We had started talking about Winter Quarters, which this show maintained in the Carolinas. I had started online job hunting at the library, filling out applications and leaving resumes in the towns nearby, while checking the housing classifieds. As much as I wanted the mission to continue, I did not want to stay on the lot, but in our own private home where I could send Rozeanna to school. I thought about the days when we were dreaming about that little white house with the picket fence, and shook my head. If God had wanted us to settle in Florida, we would have by now. I shrugged. As long as our family was together, held our faith come what may, and did what we could for people, it was enough for me.

The rain continued into the next day, causing a full cancellation of the day, and we swung the door open, grateful for the fresh air and the cool temperatures that followed. We took a few pictures of John's shoes, which I insisted he kept outside to air out, filled with water. The rain was causing some of the worst flooding in history.

On Wednesday, I brought my friend to the hospital, and much to everyone's surprise, found the source of her recent illness. She was almost three months pregnant! I congratulated her, though she looked doubtful a few moments. How could anyone take a baby on the road? We were horrified when the hospital staff told her that they would not be able to take a sonogram because she didn't have insurance. And she was a carnie.

"Maybe I should abort it," she said. I stopped her, horrified, and talked with her for the next hour in the hopes that she would change that thinking. This was a blessing in my eyes. I was told I would never have any, and the Lord gave me three beautiful angels. In the end, the talk we had inspired her, and got her thinking that maybe she could make amends with her folks. An argument with them was what brought her out to the show in the first place. I nodded, and told her I would be beside her, every step of the way, if she wished.

Thursday came, and I was excited. It was the day before my birthday, I was going to turn the Big 4-0, and our friends were planning a simple party with my favorite, barbequed chicken, and some cake. The rain had stopped and I gave the kids a bath in a wash bucket, because the shower in our trailer was broken. I pretended it was the old days, and remembered my grandfather telling us that was how he took a bath as a child. I took Rozeanna and Hunter out for a walk on the midway before opening. There was plenty of pavement, so I allowed her to ride her bike. It was a little odd, watching a child grow up in the midst of all this, but I knew with the right guidance, she and Hunter would be fine. We planned to buy a trailer, and I planned to take lessons so I could home school both kids. Who knew, maybe one day, we could return to the old days of the carnival, when school actually was held on the site, and the fair was a family-oriented place to live. That night I received a special bonus. Confederate Railroad, one of my favorite country bands, was performing for free. I was standing there with Rozeanna and Hunter, right in the front, when Roze ran up to the stage and started dancing to one of the band's signature songs. Before I knew it, the lead singer had held out his hand to this adorable little girl, and my daughter danced on stage to the beat. Afterward, we took pictures with the entire band, and Roze had them in stitches of laughter as she sweetly asked for both hands and all her fingers to be signed. Another wonderful event that day was the chorus of sweet voices singing hymns in the office tent, with Rozeanna joining right in.

I also watched as Rozeanna, being ever so polite, tried to measure kids at one of the rides, the same way her father does at his. She had that same regretful look when she told one little boy, "Oh, you might be too short!" Happily, the parents just laughed, and took it in stride.

The problem with planning ahead is the fact that we sometimes lose sight of the present, and the possible danger that's lurking. On my birthday around noon, I returned with Mark from a quick trip to the grocery store. He was kind enough to buy the chicken, and we borrowed a grill to cook it on. My pregnant friend was on her way over with a cake. She'd made me smile earlier by singing "Happy Birthday" to me on my cell phone. The Pastor, my sister, Amber, Joseph and Arlene called, too, with jokes about my being over the hill and other cracks that come with that age.

Rozeanna was playing with bubbles, and Hunter, after careful inspection for any mud and the horrid ants, was allowed to crawl in the small circle of ground between our steps and the end of the other bunks. It was this action that started all of hell breaking loose.

The pregnant girl, whose children had been taken away and who eyed mine with open hostility, started making her way toward us, with a black look on her face that set a number of people running in our direction.

Our laughter stopped short as her shadow darkened the ground, and we all glanced up.

"I don't want that baby crawling on the ground," she growled. "There could be sewer water there!"

I stood up, as did John, and scooped Hunter off the ground.

"We checked it, " I said, gently as I could. I knew what this girl was capable of, and the look on her face suggested she was in the mood to do something rash.

In the blink of an eye she reached out for Rozeanna. She snatched her up, sneering.

"I'm tired of seeing you with your kids," she growled. "I'm going to take them away from you, like I had mine taken from me!"

And she turned to flee with our daughter, tucked under her arm, screaming.

I screamed too, and was handing Hunter to John to give chase, when out of nowhere, Mark, my friend, and a few others who aligned themselves with us appeared behind the girl. She bumped right into them. Mark snatched Rozeanna out of her hands.

"*Who do you think you are, touching this kid?*" Mark screamed, and a shouting match began, with some carnies holding me back, Hunter crying, and my pregnant friend bringing Roze over to us.

The commotion brought the main supervisor over on a scooter, to see what the fuss was about. Things were quickly explained. It might have gone well, except for the arrival of one of the ticket sellers. She, with a few of her minions, came to join the melee, saying she had seen me endanger the children on a number of occasions.

"That's it!" cried the main supervisor. "Pack your bags, John, and your family's. You are *done*. It's not safe for these kids to be here anymore." He then told John if he "stashed" his family somewhere, he could come back to work.

Many who had come to join the fray on the girls' side laughed and cracked jokes. Something inside of me broke, and I started screaming at the top of my lungs over John's insistence I hush. At a frantic pace he and others packed our car, to leave once again,.

Angels truly were among us that day. Only God knows what could have happened to our daughter if the woman had made off with her. We were grateful for our friends who were concerned enough to follow her, and come to our defense.

We went to a hotel that night, one that offered a special rate for three days. We took the deal, because we had to figure out where the heck we were going to go. I had calmed down, and stated that somehow, someway, God would have the answer, and we would have a place to go to at the end of the three days.

An answer did come on the third day, and as is the case with many prayers, it was not the answer I wished for. It was an invitation from John's father to come to Pennsylvania. We had lived there before moving to Florida, but the lack of jobs made Pennsylvania the last place on the earth I wanted to be. I protested vehemently, until my wonderful husband cupped my face between his hands and kissed me.

"Jackie.... Look at it this way. Maybe, just maybe, God

needs us up there," he said.

I consented, and we packed the car again, driving on to our new home up north. The ministry, for now, was over.

Epilogue

September, 2010. As I sit on the steps of our little rental house, watching Rozeanna and Hunter ride their scooters in front of me on our dead-end street, I reflect on the day that we left, almost one year ago.

We spent seven months with John's dad, who can be difficult at times. To increase our stress, his father's housemate was a person whom trouble seemed to follow, another reason I did not want to come to Pennsylvania.

But I am so glad now, that God knows what is better for us than we do, and that we came.

I have always had two dreams, to be well-known for my photography, and for my writing. I hope to be an author one day. Not twenty-four hours after our arrival, God granted me a gift in the form of my first-ever freelance writing position as a correspondent for the county newspaper. A few months later, John got in touch with his old boss in New Jersey, about two hours away, and started working. Roze started school and is adjusting well, loving every minute. We also managed to put her into ballet classes, and her first recital was in May, 2010.

My friends, Amber and Arlene, came to Pennsylvania for the event with their children, and we managed to squeeze in trips to New York, Amish Country, and the

Hershey's Chocolate Factory, too.

At the end of June, I visited a friend in the next town, attending one of the many church festivals with the children. There, just across the street from the church, stood a tiny white two-story, for rent at a reasonable price. I went over to look at it, and Roze asked if this was the house that she saw in her dream. I blinked in surprise, asking for details. She told me that she had asked God for a house of her own. She was not happy living at Grandpa's. She wanted her own room, instead of sharing a bed with me and Hunter. John slept on a loveseat.

I told her, well, the only way to know if something is from God is to ask him. She then bowed her little head and said,

"Lord, please let me know if this is my Princess House. I would really like it to be," she said.

The faith of a child…so simple and sweet. For the next two weeks that was all she talked about, until I packed her, her brother and a bunch of things in the car, and drove there. She shrieked in delight, watching me unlock the door with the key. Yes, it was a rental, but the landlord may consider putting it up for sale some day. We'd like to buy it, God willing. Honesdale, PA is a nice little town with a population of five thousand, with a park three blocks from our home. Everything is close by, and the wholesome feeling of yesteryear is here, from the Mayberry-like Main Street shops to the many events throughout the year for families and tourists alike, making this a decent place to raise the kids. We are only ninety minutes from New York and those we love in Jersey.

We have also been blessed upon our arrival by the association of a wonderful church, run by the incredible Pastor, Patricia "Pat" Lee. She presides over one congregation, divided into two churches. We were accepted immediately into the congregation, and happily attend church there. If it were not for their love, kindness, and support, we may not have survived that winter.

Hunter was also baptized at Sterling. In October of 2010, our fantastic church Christian rock group, called The Forgiven Band, threw one of their many benefits for needy families. We were one of the recipients, and thanks to the kindness of strangers, Hunter now has his first bed.

Since moving into the house I was blessed with a bonus, a visit from my father and my sister. They made the short trip to see us at our new home. I am glad for the peace between us.

Things are still touch and go for us. I was laid off my position at the newspaper right after moving in. After working for a local advertising company and a local magazine, my contract ended, and we are once again a one income family.

John is still away, but at least he comes home on Friday nights to spend the weekend with his family. I don't know how things will go in the winter when work slows down, though. For now, I am grateful to God for every time he comes home safe to us.

I haven't seen Joe for a year and a half, and I miss him. We do talk on the phone, however, and he finally is getting a computer, so I can talk to him online.

Hunter will be two soon, and I have signed him up an early home-based Head Start program. He loves going to school, and will be ready by the time he is able to take the bus to class next year when he turns three.

My mother-in-law still is in our lives, coming up to

visit or inviting us to her house at least once a month. She lives nearly three hours away in New Jersey. But I am grateful that she got to know me last summer, and she adores her grandchildren. I value our friendship and relationship greatly.

I am forever grateful for my sister of the heart, Amber, who has been a true friend to the end, and my dear sister in Christ, Lakendra, my friend and fellow journalist, who lives in Texas. Her encouragement is an inspiration to me. I have made many new friends, one of whom, Stacy, babysits when I need to run an errand. It was her help that made it possible to get the house straightened out so quickly. Mr. Wayne is another gentleman whose company we enjoy. Another friend, Carla, has a girl Roze's age, and they are in ballet together. I am grateful for these people and the others God has put into my life.

John was also right about God's needing us in Pennsylvania. My second assignment involved covering the local library. In a conversation with the president of the library about recent deep budget cuts, I suggested an art auction fund raiser, like I had seen in Orlando. It was unheard of in this town, but the president liked the idea and called me in January to discuss it. A committee was formed, and in August, 2010, the first Pocono Art Extravaganza, presented by the fantastic *Connections* Magazine and Bold Gold Media group was held at Ehrhardt's Waterfront Resort on Lake Wallenpaupack, raising $9,400. I hope it turns into an annual event.

Through the church, we have given as well as received. Inspired by a recent sermon, another friend of the congregation and I are starting a ministry for moms and babies by making blankets and clothes for them. We are also putting together a list of resources for them to use.

As for Christ for Carnies, many would say it was a failure in the end. It all depends on how you look at things, I guess. We didn't raise a lot of funds, or have the ministry spread nationwide.

But if you look at it the way we do, that for a while, God used us as his instruments of peace, that for a while many people were moved to help a forgotten group of people in America's backyard, that we saved a few souls and planted the seeds of God's word in others, then the mission was a success.

We do keep in contact with a few of the friends that we made, and it's a wonderful feeling to hear the difference you have made in someone's life. Some of the carnies have gone home and back to school in the hopes of bettering their lives. Some have reconciled with their parents. Just as in the movie, *Pay It Forward*, John and I hope that the seeds we and the churches planted will grow, and make a difference in more lives down the road.

Christ for Carnies is on hold for now; it is not dead. But who knows? Things come full circle, I believe, and if there is anything to continue, God will lead us back that way and we'll do what we need to do. Christ was there for Carnies, for all of us, and has never left.

I don't know if Honesdale is where we are meant to be, but I took it as a good sign when John drove up, ready to enjoy the weekend with his family and called me over to his work truck.

"I have something for you," he said, giving me that grin I both love and infuriates me at the same time.

"What's that?" I asked.

"Well, I was cleaning out a house, and got all of these.

Mom, had a different piece that I think will make a great gate," he told me, flipping back a blanket to reveal a special pile of lumber.

I cried with joy and hugged him tight as I kissed him, thanking God. The kids grabbed hold of each leg and let out a whoop of joy. Wasting no time at all, John, the kids, and I got to work unloading the wood to put up my little white picket fence.

Links

Here are some wonderful links for you to check out. Please remember the smallest kindness makes the biggest difference, and it starts with you and you community.

www.avventurapress.com
www.amazon.com
http://christforcarnies.weebly.com
http://jacquelyndienst.weebly.com
www.christforcarnies.blogspot.com

Florida Links:
http://www.deltonafl.gov/
http://www.sanfordfl.gov/index.html
http://www.orlandoinfo.com/
http://www.cityoffortpierce.com/
http://www.covb.org/ - Vero Beach Fl

Virginia Links:
http://www.thehrcc.com/go/hrcc-webroot

New Jersey Links:
http://www.twp.woodbridge.nj.us/

New York Links:
http://www.iloveny.com/
http://www.statuecruises.com/

West Virginia Links:
http://en.wikipedia.org/wiki/Gerrardstown,_West_Virginia

Tennessee Links:
http://www.lebanontn.org/default.aspx
http://www.fiddlersgrove.org/component/jevents/month.calendar/2011/01/29/
http://www.memphistravel.com/

Georgia Links:
http://www.visitlawrenceville.com/
http://www.cabbagepatchkids.com/about/tour/

Pennsylvania Links:
http://www.visithonesdalepa.com/
www.boldgoldmedia.com
www.wayneindependent.com
http://www.wnep.com/
http://ryanleckey.com/tag/wnep-tv/
Search for hamlin family fun days on
    http://ryanleckey.com/leckey-live-videos/

Massachusetts Links:
http://www.valleyvisitor.com/

A Few Links of Interest:
http://www.examiner.com/la-in-scranton/a-pastors-wedding
http://www.examiner.com/la-in-scranton/meet-the-forgiven-band
www.theforgivenband.com
http://www.buildabear.com/
Check out their huggable ideas to help and other ways to give back: http://www.buildabear.com/shopping/contents/content.jsp?catId=400002&id=700013
    http://www.buildabear.com/shopping/contents/content.jsp?catId=400002&id=700008

Thank you for reading this book. I hope our story has inspired you. Remember—the smallest kindness can change a life, and it only takes a moment of your time. As for me and mine, we will continue to help those we can and pray for those we can't, and always keep the Lord in our hearts.
God Bless.

For information about bulk sales and
other Avventura Press titles, email
lee@avventurapress.com

Contact the author at jackie@avventurapress.com

WNEP TV Personality Ryan Leckey covered the 2nd annual Hamlin Family Fun Days hosted by the Sterling and Hollisterville UMC in July 2010. His co-host Hunter is now an outgoing, energetic, two year old. Special thanks to Ryan Leckey for photo permission.

Rozeanna on a model shoot for a local photographer. She wants to act, model, dance, and play guitar.

My three angels

www.ingramcontent.com/pod-product-compliance
Lightning Source LLC
Chambersburg PA
CBHW032359040426
42451CB00006B/65